"I feel like I was just given the secret recipes! This is a true gold mine of information for training professionals looking to design and deliver engaging sessions that drive results. The innovative and creative approach is a masterful blend of art, science and going with the flow. It is an invaluable resource I will refer back to again and again."

—Kathy Simpson, Manager, U.S. Sales & Global Business Unit Learning + Development, Nike

"What makes this so successful is that Julie knows how to connect at an emotional, visceral level with anyone who has ever facilitated—including those who have felt terrified by it. Unlike many books taking a mechanical approach to facilitation, here you learn from the years of experience Julie and her colleagues have amassed using non-traditional sensibilities—improv, story telling, images, bent paperclips, metaphor—to harness the full energies of a group of participants. Like any great cookbook in your kitchen, this will soon be heavily marked up, crumpled and ragged from use by anyone serious about improving as a facilitator."

—Scott Dawson, Dean, School of Business Administration, Portland State University

"Warning: Don't be fooled by how fast and easy a read this is (a 3-hour plane ride was sufficient). Whether you are an aspiring facilitator, a CEO or just make a lot of presentations, Julie's insightful observations make these recipes extremely effective. Her knowledge of what makes us tick is astounding and acutely accurate.

Having experienced these techniques first-hand, I know the recipes activate an audience, improve the outcome, are fun to be part of and more fun to practice (even for a control freak like me)."

—Mike Doherty, President, Cole & Weber United

"I read this brimming-with-insights book and said, 'Wow.' It lets you see facilitation as an art form—an accessible, practice-able, playful and change-producing art form. Wow."

—Karen Dawson, facilitator, executive coach, and Banff Centre Leadership Development faculty member

"This certainly beats Julie's first cooking project: when she was six, roasting marshmallows on a lightbulb."

—Susan MacKinnon, Julie's mother

Health Warning : Using this cookbook may result in standing-room-only conditions.

THE DEEPER, FUNNER FACILITATION COOKBOOK

Keep them on the edge of their seats and propel real change

The Deeper, Funner Facilitation Cookbook

Written with a sense of adventure by Julie Sheldon Huffaker. Illustrated by Gary Hirsch while sunning on a Mexican beach. Insightfully edited by Amy Veltman, and keenly proofed by Catherine Harold. Thoughtfully designed by Jen Viviano. Deep gratitude to Leslie Bevan, Cookbook Widow, who served up meals and opinions with generosity and endless patience. Additional, essential input and inspiration from many. Thank you all.

The Deeper, Funner Facilitation Cookbook:
Keep them on the edge of their seats and propel real change

ISBN13: 978-0-615-28682-2

Published by On Your Feet
Portland, Oregon, USA
www.oyf.com

Printed in the United States.

The Table (of Contents)

COOKING DEEPER, FUNNER MEETINGS

At the evening cocktail party launching the event, we worked our way around the bar overlooking Monterey Bay. What we found was a group of forty CIOs drinking Maker's Mark over the kind of small talk that characterizes so many business gatherings—about the flight in, the weather, the golf courses nearby. These information technology leaders were from large U.S. organizations spanning industries as varied as healthcare, retail, real estate, defense, and even the U.S. military.

Our client, the sponsor of the gathering, clinked on his glass and introduced us as the facilitation team. He highlighted Tobey's experience at Apple, mine at Starbucks, and the fact that our consulting clients were companies just like—and including—theirs. Then he passed the baton to us.

We'd been asked to facilitate a session with these leaders to create a shared vision for online technology in the future. Our client was nervous, because he'd invited CIOs from competing companies and because he knew the future-casting would be a stretch for any creative team, let alone the linear thinkers in this room. He'd originally imagined a safe, round-table-discussions-between-drinks-and-golf sort of gathering. But we had a different idea.

"We know one of the reasons you're here is to network and learn from each other," we said, "And we also know learning happens through relationship. We'll start by giving you a different way to get to know each other. We want you to tell the stories of your names." I began with my own high school nickname, Crusher, from the infamous soccer game when, with a single kick, I scored the winning goal for the opposing team and broke our star forward's femur. They looked at us unbelievingly for a moment, then divided awkwardly into pairs to tell their own stories. They began to lean in, listening intently to each other. There was laughter, and the noise level grew. We looked at each other and breathed a sigh of relief.

"To set the stage, we're going to break you into teams and give you an impossible task," we told them next. We gave each team a question about current technology trends and concerns. Their task: to design a research strategy that would get an answer to their question from every other person in the room, implement the strategy, analyze the results, and plan a short and memorable presentation communicating what they learned. Then we told them the impossible part: for each stage, they would have exactly three minutes. They groaned.

But they attacked the task with vigor, and this time the noise level skyrocketed. Just before the presentations, we called for attention. "How much do you think audience members remember of what they hear?" we asked. They guessed about 15%. "What they hear and see?" we asked. 50%. "How much of what they hear, see, and do?" A whopping 75%. "Your job is to make sure everyone remembers your presentation," we told them. "Take a few extra minutes to make it a hear-see-do presentation."

The presentations were informative. They were also hilarious. After the last one, the group leapt to their feet to give each other a roaring ovation. "What do you want us to do next?" they asked. Tobey and I laughed. "Drink!" we told them.

The next morning, we got them back on their feet. We knew the key to keeping them engaged was to give real-world value immediately. We also knew these hard-core technology experts often struggled to get their organizations to see technology as a competitive advantage, and worth investing in. Their ability to influence back at the office impacted their success adopting the kinds of innovations we were here to work on.

"Now we'll do something to help you get more from your time here," we told them. We put them in pairs again, designating one tapper and one listener. The tapper tapped out the beats of a well-known song for his listener, who had to guess what it was. (This exercise, based on research done by Elizabeth Newton at Stanford, is described by Chip and Dan Heath in their magnificently useful book, *Made to Stick*.) The exercise highlights the gap between tappers' belief that their tapping is easily understandable (they estimate the chance their listener will get the song at about 50%) and the actual ability of the listeners to guess accurately with such limited information (~2.5%). As one CIO put it, "What is it about Jingle Bells you don't understand?!?"

"You're experts in your field and industries," we explained. "When you're humming the song in your head, you tap and assume everyone else is getting the full picture. To get the most value from these two days, your job is to hum out loud, and ask others to hum out loud, to get as much of your expertise and perspective on the table as possible." They nodded thoughtfully as

they took their seats. "I think I do a hell of a lot of tapping back at the office," someone commented ruefully. The group laughed with recognition.

Tobey and I walked through the agenda and then pulled on black-and-white striped referee shirts and whistles. "Don't get too comfortable in your chairs," we cautioned. "Our job is to keep things moving." We launched into a sequence of mixed-industry breakouts with reflection and discussion in between. As the rounds progressed, we used a variety of techniques to name external trends, identify strategic 3- to 5-year corporate goals and priorities, and capture the CIO's top needs and considerations pursuing those goals.

Over lunch, a series of speakers gave short teaching pieces on five cutting-edge technologies and how early adopters were inventively using them. The day ended with CIOs rotating through a station for each online technology, working with the experts and each other to envision possible applications.

At the bar that evening, three CIOs waved us over. They insisted on buying us drinks, sharing their appreciation for the day. Then, they pointed out something we missed: using cross-industry groups in the very first exercise, looking at external trends, had diluted the outcome. "It would help us to see those trends by industry, so we can compare what we're experiencing with our peers and competitors." They were right. The next morning, we announced an agenda change and began with their version of the exercise, which produced rich and satisfying discussion.

The day progressed. The CIOs developed possible technologies further. Voting with their feet, they self-organized around the one they believed had the most potential to create competitive advantage for their enterprise. In these final teams, we gave them their most ambitious assignment yet: to develop and "show" a short, live-action documentary from the future (read: they had to act everything out, with props they made themselves). Their "footage" had to show how the future technology worked, chronicle three giant steps needed to deploy it at their company, and show how they overcame a significant obstacle. The final take was of the technology being used in a way that created significant competitive advantage for their organization.

As they worked to physically bring their film segments to life, their excitement and their idea generation accelerated: "What if it had special functionality that . . . " "One thing we haven't thought about is . . . " "Try this—wouldn't it really help that user there if . . . "

When they finally screened their documentaries, the CIOs had fleshed out features, functionality and usage scenarios far beyond expectations. Their vignettes brought these to life in a no-holds-barred kind of way: they programmed their cell phones to mimic new functionality, built things out of cardboard, climbed on chairs, and dove under tables.

Frankly, we were blown away. All of us—the client, CIOs, Tobey, and me. Sure, we designed the session, but we didn't expect the CIOs to do so much with it.

"What surprised me," offered one CIO in the final debriefing, "was that I could work so comfortably and creatively with my peers—and competitors —in such a short time." He paused. "Imagine what would happen if we got together like this more often."

Cooking deeper, funner meetings

Afterwards, driving north through the avocado fields on the way to the airport, Tobey turned to me. "You have a real point of view about how to design sessions so they really work. You should write this down," he said. "Call it the 'Deeper, Funner Meeting Cookbook' or something."

I thought back to a terrifying evening years ago—the night between the two days of the very first strategic planning session I ever facilitated. It wasn't my first session; I'd trained front-line coffee employees and moderated numerous focus groups as a market researcher. But this was my first paid gig as an independent consultant working with a leadership team. And at the end of the first day, all we had were some clay lumps decorated with pipe cleaners and glitter to represent where the company wanted to go. The client was off getting drunk in the bar. I had no idea how to pull this thing off.

Every cell in my body, however, knew what I wanted to do. Pack up, get in the rental car, and drive.

So as Tobey sped down that California highway and suggested I write down some of what we had done, I thought how helpful it would have been to have a handbook for cooking a great facilitated session 10 years ago, before I sat staring down those pipe cleaners.

At On Your Feet, the consulting group with which I do my facilitating and learning, we use highly experiential methods—including the unlikely resource of improvisational theater—to help teams and leaders with communication, creativity, and change. We are constantly experimenting all over the world with new ways to create learning experiences that nail the business result, propel individual self-awareness, and are ridiculously fun and inspiring. Beyond the ways we've used improv tools explicitly to address a specific client need, we've also used them invisibly, as our own working method for facilitating. Over time, we realized what an enormous difference that made for the groups we worked with (and for us as facilitators). Our clients asked us to teach them, so we began offering 1- to 3-day improv-based facilitation and presentation courses. That allowed us to learn even more, because it forced us to sit down and really understand what we were already doing instinctively.

This is not to say the job is easy. Human beings and groups are messy. Objectives can be slippery. You try things and they fail, and you're not even sure why. As a facilitator, you may be working with an energized, creative team or unfairly made the object of their lost faith. You may be collaborating with a wise, development-minded leader, or unconsciously brought in to fill the leadership gap in a group of people who just can't seem to find a way to be nice to each other. You may be asked to address business issues, while the real barriers are the deeper fears and needs of the human beings around the table. For me, there are few things more satisfying than the breakthrough moments when everyone walks out changed.

My own learning itch around this work comes honestly. I am the daughter of a psychiatrist who worked with the criminally insane, and I was trained as a cultural anthropologist. I am endlessly curious about human and organizational dynamics (sometimes annoyingly so—just ask my partner). These dynamics all come together in the room when you're facilitating. And people can be pretty amazing. They surprise me constantly.

So this cookbook is my offering for team leaders, business line managers, internal human resources and learning & development professionals, external management, marketing and organizational development consultants. If you plan and facilitate standing staff meetings, offsites, or ad hoc problem-solving or brainstorming sessions that last from 90 minutes to two days, this book is designed to make your life easier and your sessions deeper, more fun, and even more successful.

You might be reading this because you want sessions to be even more engaging and impactful. You might be looking for ways to dial up real attitude and behavior change (instead of having the exact same meeting every 6 months). Or you might simply be a learning junkie like me. Regardless, if you have an inkling there's more to facilitation than scented markers and sticky notes, we, your fellow revolutionaries, have a few ideas. (Throughout the cookbook, I'll shift fluidly between "I" and "we" depending on whether I'm speaking from collective On Your Feet experience or my own exploration. Note: Nothing is in here that we haven't tried ourselves and found to be especially satisfying.)

You'll get the most from this cookbook if you have some basic facilitation experience. It helps if you've been a participant in facilitated group gatherings like strategic planning or training sessions, too, so you can identify with what it's like to be on the receiving end. Those of you who are very comfortable facilitating will be able to grab tidbits that fit with questions you've been noodling on and use them immediately. If you're newer, remember that this is a practice. There's no substitute for learning firsthand from your own experimentation in the kitchen.

Not granny's gentle pie

If it sounds like this cookbook might be all sugar and sprinkles, Betty Crocker aprons, and spatula metaphors, don't be fooled.

This is more like a cross between *Cook's Illustrated* and *The Anarchist's Cookbook*, with a good mixture of pancake batter and acetone stuck to the pages. My goal is to blow up a few assumptions about how far people will go outside their typical comfort zone in a business meeting, and what's possible when you help them go there. At On Your Feet, we are interested in experimenting with co-creation and learning through what's happening in the moment, and we're not afraid to break a few rules to discover a better way of doing things. Deeper, more fun meetings are delicious and deeply satisfying, for your audience and for you.

A cookbook based on improvisation may seem like a contradiction. One of the most interesting aspects of improv is that, like truly great cooking, it's spontaneous but not random. A short set of simple guidelines enables extraordinary freedom and creativity. Facilitating in this way does take a little chutzpah now and then. But we suspect you wouldn't be reading this if you didn't already have that.

A seven-course meal

Our experimenting over the years has evolved into a structure—a series of seven basic courses, if you will—that we find creates deeper, more impactful experiences. We use these in virtually all of our facilitated sessions.

This cookbook contains a "recipe," complete with cooking tips and examples, for each course.

#1 **Start with the ending**—Learn how and why to get very clear about what you want to walk out with, and let the rest flow from there.

#2 **Start with the beginning**—Get tips for using the first 5 to 15 minutes to get the group leaning forward and engaged, willing to go with you, and collaborating productively with each other.

#3 **Get the head nod**—Make your audience feel seen and understood by mapping out their needs and issues. Get them to fill in any gaps.

#4 **Show the value (not tell it or sell it)**—Show your audience the value they will get from a session with something visual, vivid, and/or story-based. This recipe can provoke emotional reactions and increase their motivation.

#5 Create a roomful of co-facilitators—Early on, engage the group in sharing responsibility for their experience and their learning by giving them a task and connecting the work to their real stuff. But beware: this is not your mama's agenda-setting.

#6 Make real change—We would call this the entrée, but unlike some main courses, this never works as a one-dish meal. For the change to stick, the previous steps are just as important even if they don't take up as much time. We'll provide ideas and methods to facilitate both the practical work—like information-sharing, brainstorming, and decision making—and the emotional ahas that drive real understanding, commitment and new action. Included are tips for handling picky eaters that resist, interrupt, and throw food at the table, and dealing with them skillfully in a way that maintains connection and serves the needs of the group.

#7 End with something sticky—Make it a meal they'll rave about with a clear, engaging recap, interactive ahas and takeaways, accountable follow-through, and something delicious in the final moments.

Some of these dishes you'll cook in advance, store in the freezer and pull out the day of. Others you'll assemble real-time while your guests are hanging out in the kitchen. Most are simple, with just a few ingredients, while others are like bread—easy to learn but they take time and practice to truly master. You don't have to include all of these dishes all of the time to make a balanced meal (although it's worth saying we usually do.)

Try it!

The best way to learn new stuff is to practice on something real. So before you go any further, take a moment. Think of a meeting or session you're facilitating soon or have recently done.

At the end of each of the seven courses, we'll give you prompts to help you try the recipe on your real stuff. You know your own facilitation style and needs best; your job is to discover what's most useful to you, and experiment to make it your own. If you do this for each course, when you finish the cookbook you should have a near-complete, really good design ready to use.

Now. Pull out your mini blow torch.

TREASURE

PANTRY ESSENTIALS

Here are a few tools and ingredients that will enable you to follow the recipes in this book. They're also just good things to have around.

Willingness to do things differently

The American cook and author Julia Child once burned a whole turkey to a blackened, smoking crisp on a public television science show. (She was trying to make the point that everything is made of carbon. The turkey obviously was.) She almost set the studio kitchen on fire with that bird, and just laughed her head off as she pulled it from the oven.

One of Julia's mantras was, "Never be afraid to try things in a different way." (She also said, "Always use plenty of butter," which I find equally useful.) She wouldn't want any of us to rigidly measure out perfect tablespoons alongside everyone else. A recipe is a starting place. Be willing to try different things, different ways.

A slab of improv

Improvisers take the stage with no script, no plan, and only themselves and their fellow improvisers as resources. In a state of uncertainty and constant change, their job is to collaborate to create an engaging story.

Blinded by the lights in front of a live audience and charged with creating an engaging performance from nothing, most of us would fight, freeze, or flee. Improvisers train themselves to do just the opposite. They use a set of practices that enable them to actually enjoy the uncertainty and, collaborating as a group, find new information and possibilities in it. (Aside from the practical benefits, improv is also ridiculously fun.)

Like improv, facilitation is an inherently co-creative art form. As a facilitator, your job is to help create an overarching "story" (a new plan, new ideas, or new understanding) that engages and satisfies your audience. While you may come in with a picture in your head of what you want to have happen, you must quickly release it and skillfully use what's happening in the moment—including what comes flying in from left field—to move the action forward.

The practices improvisers use on stage are a great help to facilitators. Here's a CliffsNotes description of them:

- Notice more. Slow things down to stretch the senses, reach beyond day-to-day filters, and take in more information than you normally would. When you notice more about the situation, the other people in it, and yourself, you have more to work with. (How much are you noticing these days? Go to http://www.dothetest.co.uk/. Based on research originally done at the University of Illinois' Memory & Cognition Unity, it's pretty cool stuff.)
- Be willing to be changed. Most of us have been told at one time or another that we should listen better, but this instruction is confusing. What are you supposed to do, exactly? We think it's more helpful to focus on showing that you're changed by what you hear. Improvisers consciously let go of their own agendas and let themselves be changed by the offers around them to better serve the story. Refusing to be changed is safe. Letting yourself be changed is risky. It takes you somewhere new, uncharted, and out of your control.
- See everything as an offer. In improv speak, an offer is anything you can do something with. Offers can be verbal, physical, or emotional. Coughing, crossing their legs, apologizing for being late, shivering, challenging the process . . . your audience is making offers all the time. For an improviser, offers aren't good or bad. They are simply something you can use.

Offers are important, so we'll spend a bit more time with them.

What can you do with an offer? On stage, there are only two options: accept or block. Imagine we were coworkers, and I came up to you with this offer: "Let's paint the office blue." Here are some possible responses you might give:

> *Great idea! Let's change the carpet, too.* OR
>
> *The boss hates blue. Let's paint it yellow instead.* OR
>
> No. OR
>
> *Is there a good place to get a cup of coffee around here?*

To accept an offer means to recognize it and do something with it. Accepting offers puts money in the emotional bank account between two people. It builds relationship and generates new possibilities about what might happen.

To block an offer means to not recognize it, or not do something with it. Blocking offers takes money out of the bank account. It detracts from the relationship and limits the possibilities by keeping things the same (or trying to).

So let's look at those again. Accept or block?

Great idea! Let's change the carpet, too. (Accept: recognizes and does something with it.)

The boss hates blue. Let's paint it yellow instead. (Tricky for some, but accept: recognizes the offer and does something with it. Accepting does not mean agreeing with the idea—simply recognizing it and doing something with it that moves the story forward.)

No. (Big fat block! Recognizes the offer, but doesn't do anything with it.)

Is there a good place to get a cup of coffee around here? (Again, a block: doesn't recognize the offer at all.)

A huge piece of the art of facilitation is noticing more about the offers the group is making in the moment. This also means finding a way to accept them—including being willing to be changed by them if that serves the group's best interests.

This all sounds fine—until something unexpected or irritating happens. Someone asks a question you can't answer, ratholes, has sidebar conversations, or pulls out their BlackBerry. To learn more about skillfully accepting offers like these, make sure to read the recipe for the fifth course of the meal, "Make Real Change."

Last comment about improv: It's basically open source. Everyone is always changing things even when they don't mean to, and that's where new, interesting discoveries come from. By and large, you can't "own" anything in the improv tradition. How could you? That would be a bit like owning a piece of life itself. The improv way is to credit where you learned something or who you learned it from, knowing this may or may not be the original source. I've tried to do that here. If I missed crediting someone for their brilliant idea, I'm sorry. Please let me know so I can do better next time.

A tool kit with an appetite

It helps to have a hungry toolkit—a growing collection of exercises, games, books, and stories, that wants to be fed. The end of the cookbook includes several books and websites we find particularly helpful to help you nourish yours.

An image library

Our spirited colleague Kay Scorah of Dublin (an On YOur Feet collaborator and the genius of consultancy Have More Fun, Get More Done) started us off with our image libraries. Rather than buy an expensive laminated kit, Kay just collects wads of photos—a range of subjects, moods, and textures—which she scans and prints on letter-size paper on her color printer at home. She uses them in many different ways in her sessions. At On Your Feet, we each keep a store of images and add as we go along. Like the photo of Brad's VW Golf crumpled on the curb outside the building where we did a State of Oregon job. We walked out and it was just sitting there, thoroughly smashed by a plumbing truck. I'll point out a few of the many ways you might use an image library as we go along.

Tape dots

Run, don't walk, to get these. An architectural client turned us on to them. You can find them at any drafting supply store: a petite box of round, low-adhesive tape dots that affix wall charts in a snap.

HOW TO ARRANGE THE KITCHEN

These are some tips for arranging space (and time) to get the most out of a session.

Interactive room setup

Our typical setup for 6 to 25 people is a semi-circle of chairs facing a long wall. On the wall, we post a series of oversized wall charts. Notice that there is no boardroom table and this is not the traditional conference-style U. There are no tables in front of or behind participants. (This sometimes makes them feel exposed, with no other alternative but to engage—just the way we like it.)

Even if we've sent schematics in advance, we often walk into a venue and find banquet rounds or one of those huge, mahogany boardroom tables in the middle of the room. With that in mind, we always arrive early, ready to move furniture.

No tables means no laptops, and direct and ongoing interaction with us as facilitators and with each other. No tables also means lots of flexibility to move around, have a large interactive space, reconfigure into small groups, etc. Our standard setup includes two easels with Post-it pads up front, too—one in each corner.

Storyboarding with wall charts

We take our cue from Edward Tufte, the "Galileo of visual information display" (http://www.edwardtufte.com). In facilitated sessions, we try to get as much information up in front of people, visually, as possible. We create a visual storyboard of the session using our large wall charts—usually peppered with key concepts and bold illustrations. These look impressive, but they're cheap and easy; we send them over to our terrific neighborhood copy guy or make them at FedEx Kinko's on their oversized copier if we're in another city (https://printonline.fedexkinkos.com/).

When participants walk in and see these storyboards, they immediately get a sense for the steps we'll be taking. As we move through the session, we capture key takeaways, decisions, and other notes on these charts or on flip-chart paper that we stick nearby. We think this makes it easier for the group to stay on the same page (literally), and because it's so visually impactful, it makes key content and takeaways stickier. In large keynote or conference situations we do use PowerPoint, but rarely elsewhere.

To ban or not to ban? Cell phones and Berries

We take our lead on this from a client who taught us a ton about many things, Karl Zabel. Karl said with characteristic frankness: "It's valuable feedback. If they're on their cell phones, I haven't done a good job keeping them engaged, or they're not perceiving this as valuable. If they feel our session is a great use of their time, and they are fully engaged by what we're doing, they won't worry about their phones." In general, we find this to be the case.

So we don't take on the role of compliance officer about cell phone or BlackBerry use. We typically send out a pre-mail that lets people know the session will require their full focus, and they should make whatever arrangements they need to be uninterrupted. And that's the last we say about it.

It's tempting to think that the reason we don't have trouble with interruptions is that we're fascinating, witty, and attractive. What's probably closer to the truth is that we typically have everyone up and moving around so often that there is little opportunity to do anything else.

Variety and the energy curve (a change is as good as a rest)

One of the (many) things our collaborator in Spain, Rob Poynton, spends time thinking about is the energy curve of a workshop. He is interested in skillfully shifting energy from one kind to another to help the group do its best work. Where do you want high energy—but not so much that everyone gets burnt out and has nothing left for the harder tasks later? Where do they need a more reflective exercise? What's the overall curve that will end things with a spirit of can-do and optimism, versus bleary fatigue?

THE END OF OUR BEGINNING

In addition to your own imagination and willingness to take risks, the ingenuity and impact of your session designs are driven by how deeply you grok the client context and needs. No cookbook can ever substitute for expertise in organizational development, team leadership, marketing, strategy, customer service, or other topics related to the client need you've been asked to help fulfill. If you're facilitating a session with architects on improving the project management process, this doesn't mean you have to be an architect. But it is an asset to bring some understanding of common team challenges like role clarity, decision making, and delegation.

Notice more, again: Being a keen observer of your own life also helps. The most profound insight you have to offer a group struggling with conflict might be what you notice about what you did—and didn't do—last week when your neighbor's teenage son blocked your driveway with his car. Again.

#1 START WITH THE ENDING

We sat with the leaders of an innovative marketing firm, eating dark chocolate. Sexy client list. Big ideas. Always great snacks in the conference room. They'd hired hotshot young talent from a range of disciplines to fuel their unusual approach.

We need more accountability!" one of the co-founders jabbed his finger in the air. "We need people who will take things and run with them. I get called in on every little decision. We hired these people because of their track records, but I always have to jump in and fix things. We have exactly 1.5 days for this offsite, and I really need them to step up."

Stories often tell us more than the leaders can see themselves, so we asked them to tell us a few of the times when employees took accountability beautifully and executed to their standards, and others when the co-founders felt they had to jump in. The stories were revealing.

"Let's create a working set of desired outcomes for the offsite based on this conversation," we suggested. "Then, we'll chat with 5 or 6 team members to get their input—anonymous, but not confidential. We'll share a summary with you to confirm or modify the desired outcomes, and share it with everyone at the offsite as well. What do you think?"

As our team phone calls progressed, the picture got clearer. These bright young marketers didn't know when they were authorized to make decisions, and when they weren't. They'd forge ahead on a task they thought was theirs, then get their "hands slapped" for not checking in. They also described getting 11th hour feedback from the leaders, who told them "this isn't how we do it here" and radically changed creative direction. The overall lack of clarity was creating uncomfortable competition and conflict on project teams.

"Don't get me wrong," assured one employee, "Our co-founders are brilliant, and the creative results are great. But the process is frustrating. And I'm hesitant to go very far without their input."

Taking up and letting go: a classic (not to mention uncomfortable) tension between leaders and teams. Before thinking about accountability per se, they needed three important building blocks. "At the end of 1.5 days," we told the leaders, "we think your team needs to walk out with:

- A shared delegation framework (to clarify delegated tasks—including what success looks like, and anticipated check-ins)
- New tools and language for increased decision clarity (who owns what decision, and what input is needed)

- **Shared understanding of best practices for effective feedback** (to help young talent know what's on target and what's not, and to align everyday work with the firm's creative approach)

When we finished summing up our perception of their desired outcomes, they nodded and already looked relieved. They pushed a plate of chocolate truffles across the table toward us. "Let's get started."

What do we want to walk out with?

One of our cherished collaborators, Karen Dawson, was a Lieutenant Flight Commander in the Canadian Military Reserve—which may explain how she stays so fiercely focused when designing workshops. "Let's get very, very clear about what they need to walk out with," she says in her pert Vancouver Island accent. "The rest will flow from there."

If you think I'm talking about creating the agenda here, think again. This is different. I'm talking about the desired outcomes, and they come first. Desired outcomes are what you want them to walk out with—new knowledge, awareness, tools, or skills. The agenda is the how: what, specifically, you and the group will do to make sure the desired outcomes are met. (Health warning: in this cookbook, the agenda probably comes waaay later than you're used to. And that's by design.)

A good set of desired outcomes helps you get on the same page as your stakeholders. We rarely move into design until we get (convincing) agreement from our stakeholders that yes, this is absolutely what would be of value for their team.

Desired outcomes help keep you honest and on target as you design your session. If the desired outcome is "the ability to communicate perspectives in a way that encourages productive dialogue," then a lecture and a stack of handouts isn't enough. "Ability to" implies new tools, practice using them, feedback, and enough supported experience to have confidence they can do it on their own.

Desired outcomes also help you evaluate trade-offs. When someone calls at the last minute to ask, "Could we squeeze in a 30-minute market update?", look at the desired outcomes together. Does the market update support, detract, or distract?

There is a mysterious bit of magic to desired outcomes, as well. The perfect example or ideal exercise often drops into my lap a few days after I've gotten clear about them—with no effort on my part whatsoever. Establishing creative tension between where you are and where you're going draws you toward the end result like a magnet, and invites synchronicity. Quantum physicists would no doubt say a lot more about this. I say just go with it.

INGREDIENTS

Real understanding

Get clear about where your stakeholders are and where they want to be.

Nouns

Identify the new skills, knowledge, or abilities the group most needs to get traction.

Ruthless focus

Pick no more than three. (There will always be more. Be strong.)

HOW TO COOK IT

Unearth the nouns

In our experience, it makes a surprisingly big difference to frame desired outcomes as nouns (what you want to walk out with) versus verbs (what you will do during the session).

Traditional meeting agenda (verbs):		Desired outcomes—what we'll walk out with (nouns):
Review last year's goals and accomplishments	. . . becomes . . .	Shared understanding of how we did on last year's goals and new insight into what we can do differently to be even more effective next year
Discuss non-negotiables of the brand	. . . becomes . . .	List of brand non-negotiables we can use to create consistency across retail locations
Create team strategic plan	. . . becomes . . .	Vivid picture of how we want things to look 1 year from now, with quarterly milestones

Noun cheat sheet

- *New understanding of . . .*
- *Shared agreement about . . .*
- *An agreed upon plan for . . .*
- *A brainstormed list of ideas for . . .*
- *Three options for . . .*
- *New clarity about . . .*
- *New insight into . . .*
- *New tools for . . .*
- *New ability to . . .*
- *Increased confidence that . . .*
- *A clear decision about . . .*

Ruthless focus

How many desired outcomes? Here's where the ruthless focus comes in. Three (or fewer) is a good number. We could make up something to explain why we think this is true, but the bottom line is that it just seems to work best. (We cheat sometimes and add more. We always regret it.) Based on your experience and understanding of the situation, what will be most useful in helping them move forward?

Get contaminated

In a conference pre-day several years ago, a brilliant facilitator and hero of ours, Sivasailam Thiagarajan (Thiagi), baldly stated: "Never do pre-interviews. You will be contaminated."

I get what he means. As soon as your head is full of observations, interpretations and hypotheses about the group, you stop taking in what's actually happening—what's true in the moment. Your mind selectively chooses what fits with your assumptions and beliefs, and completely ignores what doesn't. This is simply how the brain works. You can't avoid it.

For most sessions, though, I want time to mull over what I'm hearing and discern the dynamics and patterns in the stakeholder's situation so I can figure out which desired outcomes hit the center of the target. I throw in the towel, go ahead, get contaminated, and do my best to notice more during the session.

In the spirit of getting past tapping, I'll do a little humming and walk through some possible approaches. To get really clear about where stakeholders are and where they want to be, I usually do one or more of the following:

1. **Talk with the leader.**

   The upside: A bird's eye view of the issue, including a greater understanding of how it's affecting the team or organizational results. You build rapport and trust. It's efficient with a low time investment.

   The downside: You may inherit the leader's blind spots; she can't tell you what she doesn't see herself. (Stories and examples help reveal the bigger picture.) You may also be perceived as the leader's "ally," and in a politicized environment, it's important to have trust and credibility with the entire team.

Some good questions to use:

- What's the result you want that you're not getting?
- What's your hunch about why you're not getting it? What do you think is missing or getting in the way for your team? An example?
- Specifically, what do you want to be different after this session? What do you want them to walk out and do? What new knowledge, understanding or ability do you want the group to have?
- What do you think your role in all of this is? How might you be contributing to the current situation?
- What haven't I asked that you think I should know?

2. Pre-interview or email the team.

The upside: A broader perspective on the issue or need; you can adjust scope based on what you hear. You build trust with the team, which increases effectiveness. Your truthful reporting of themes also increases group candor. (Interviews are anonymous but not confidential).

The downside: Requires a greater time investment. Random samples work well, but leaders will often innocently want to influence them. "Barbara would be great to talk with. I wouldn't talk to Bill; he's never fit in around here." Asking for a full list with contact info, roles, and years of experience lets you pick a diverse and unbiased sample. Warning: Email may seem like a time saver, but often needs clarification. If you hear, "Our team needs to communicate better," you still need to find out "What's an example of that?" "What does communication look like today?"

Simple but grounding questions for a team offsite are:

- Successes—What would you describe as the team's top three successes over the past year?
- Wish list—What new skill or capacity does the team need next to be successful this year?

Mystery objective

There's often something a group needs that we don't have a clue about ahead of time. They may not even know it themselves. We'll add a fourth bullet, say we'll leave it blank for now, and then check-in at the end: What else did you get from your time together-beyond the original desired outcomes-that you really needed?

3. **Diagnose in the moment.**

You'll always be doing some of this. There's only so much you can tell about a group before you see the whites of their eyes. Here are some considerations for using it as your sole strategy, and walking in cold.

The upside: A good solution if you're short on prep time, budget, or access to the team. This route invites responding to what's happening in the moment versus acting on preconceptions.

The downside: Uses precious session time. Reduces your ability to marinate or mull over a design ahead of time. There may also be limits to how candid group members will be face-to-face.

A useful technique: An image library is handy for diagnosing on the spot. My favorite approach in this situation, again from Kay in Dublin: "Choose one image that expresses how it feels on the team right now, and a second that expresses how you long for it to feel."

Regardless of what approach you use, make sure you get down to the real challenge.

Try This

For your upcoming session, what are the desired outcomes-what do they really need to walk out with?

1.

2.

3.

Remember:

- Do you need additional perspectives beyond the leader's?
- Have you gotten down to the real challenge?
- Nouns, not verbs.

#2 START WITH THE BEGINNING

"Hi, I'm Gary Hirsch of On Your Feet. We are a collision between business and the arts, a consulting network that uses experiential methods—including techniques from improvisational theater—to help people with communication, creativity, and change. We work with many different types of organizations, from companies like Nike, Intel, GE, and Disney to a group of Zen monks outside San Francisco.

Our backgrounds are all very different. On Your Feet includes MBAs, ex-marketing executives, yoga teachers, a cultural anthropologist, and a visual artist. I do the somewhat twisted illustrations you see on our t-shirts. If you know downtown Portland at all, you may have seen the giant fish illustrations on the side of the Morrison parking garage; I did those, too.

"Now, I could stand up here and keep talking about myself, but here's one thing I know. Chances are you stopped listening to me a few minutes ago. The moment I said, 'improvisational theater,' you started wondering what I was going to make you do. When we mention improv, it usually inspires two emotions: fear and dread. What we know from experience is that the best cure is to stand up and actually do something. So please get up . . . "

Standing in a circle, the group listened to Gary explain the rules of the game. "I'm about to confirm your worst fears about what you might have to do. We are going to play a silly, ridiculous game about being a rabbit. You are going to look silly and ridiculous playing it. And your colleagues are going to look silly and ridiculous, too."

He explained the rules, then after a practice round or two, Gary stopped the action.

"I don't know this for sure, but I suspect there may be someone in the circle behind me who's rolling their eyes—internally or externally—and thinking, 'We're paying them for this crap?' You might all be thinking that. Now, of course, I am asking you to be silly and ridiculous, and that's not something you do every day at work. Not all of you, anyway. (Laughter.) It's worth taking a moment to notice what happens when we do something unusual, that might put us in an uncomfortable position. Our brains are very clever when this happens. They go to judgment. They do that to escape the discomfort of the moment. To keep us from being uncomfortable, our brains build a wall between us and what's happening, one brick at a time. 'This is a ridiculous game. They're wasting my time; I have an important job and emails piling up in my inbox. Sanj looks ridiculous playing this game. I'm going to look ridiculous playing this game. I wish I hadn't been so grumpy with my wife this morning. I shouldn't have worn these jeans; they make me look fat.'

"Before you know it, there's a wall of judgment between you and what's happening here.

"So if you know this is happening, you have a choice. You can be here physically, but stay in judgment land mentally. Or, if you're going to play a silly, ridiculous game about being a rabbit, you can commit to being here—really be the bunny.

"We can't tell you what to do. But I can tell you that we'll all know what choice you make. If you're here physically, but judging mentally, we'll see something like this." Gary showed the group a very sick and feeble bunny.

"There's one more thing you need to know. This is a competitive elimination game." There was a surprised silence, then everyone leaned in, suddenly serious. "Let's get this show going," called out one of the players.

Alternating between fierce concentration and uproarious laughter, the group played a fast-paced game down to the last rabbit. As they caught their breath at the end, Gary asked, "I'm curious. What did it take to play that game?"

They reflected: Focus and attention, the willingness to let go of self-consciousness and take risks in front of peers, rapid-fire cooperation. He nodded.

"These are some of the same qualities we see in high-performing teams. If at any moment during the day you wonder what you should be doing," said Gary, "You could do worse than to remember this list."

Meeting audience needs

To make visible all the choices we made in this opening 10 minutes, we need to go back about 10 years, when a creative firm we knew asked if we could help them be more effective during pitches. Over lunch the next day, we brainstormed what we knew from the improv stage about engaging audiences.

One thing we knew was that, generally speaking, the audience starts out wanting you to succeed. Why would they show up just to waste their time? They'll give you the benefit of the doubt for a short while, but if the thread of their attention breaks it's extremely tough to get them back.

So on the back of a napkin that day at lunch, we brainstormed a list of audience needs performers must meet, in a perilously short time, to open up audience listening and move them from giving you the benefit of the doubt to leaning forward on the edge of their seats and wanting more.

The list from our first "napkin exercise" was simple, and hasn't changed much over time. To be engaged, audiences need to:

- **Trust the driver (you)**—The audience needs to be confident in your competence so they are willing to go with you wherever you take them.
- **Know who you are (beyond titles)**—They need to know more about you than your resume; they need to know you are someone they want to spend time with.
- **Be seen**—People need to know it makes a difference that they're there. They want to feel that you get where they're coming from.
- **Know how they fit**—Audiences must know what role they're expected to play, and what it will take for them to be successful.
- **Know why they should care**—They need a reason to be invested, early on.
- **Get something of value**—Eventually, the audience needs to get something that will make their life (or their job, or that week, or just a few minutes) easier or better.
- **Be changed**—By the time they walk out, people want to be impacted as a result of their experience with you.
- **Meet other needs, specific to the group**—A hip ad agency may need to know you're not the Kumbayah people and they won't be doing trust falls off Volkswagens, for example, or an engineering team may need to know you've worked with other analytical thinkers.

Looking at the list, we saw that our most successful facilitated meetings off the stage met these requirements, too. Most interesting was that we did some heavy lifting and met the first five needs right up front. As facilitators, we know the start is so important that we invest a disproportionate amount of design time into it, and I'll spend roughly half of this cookbook focusing on it.

Remember these needs as we move into the next courses. A focus on meeting audience needs and using ongoing strategies to keep groups engaged in the moment and co-creating the experience with us shapes all of our recipes.

This is our recipe for the official beginning—the first 5 to 15 minutes of a facilitated session. In these minutes, you meet the first three audience needs: the need to trust the driver, the need to know who you are beyond titles, and the need to know how they fit.

INGREDIENTS

Trust-the-driver

Reassure the group you have something to offer that they could benefit from.

Beyond titles, personal creds

Show them a real human being they can relate to and want to be with.

Stealth norming

Create a real-time experience of the working dynamic that will get them the best results during the session: active (versus passive), co-creative, and comfortable taking risks so their ability to learn together is accelerated.

Confidence (yours) and a dash of risk (theirs)

Stretch them farther than they think they'll go.

HOW TO COOK IT

Establish trust-the-driver

When you introduce yourself (or, always better, when you are introduced by a stakeholder), it's true: it's useful to show a bit of professional leg. However, combine this with the nervousness some facilitators feel when they're up in front of a group for the first time and believe they need to prove themselves, and you might succumb to the temptation to spend the first minutes blabbing out your long resume of professional qualifications.

Think about it from the audience's perspective: Do you really want to get in the car with someone who is obsessed with impressing you with their own qualifications?

As you introduce yourself, consider:

- **What 2–3 experiences have you had that will make them feel confident you have something to offer that will benefit them**? Stick with the highlights.

- **What's your connection to the topic**? Let yourself be inspired by something that's fresh and real—perhaps a specific moment over the last few days when you got new insight into the group or subject.
- **What are you especially curious about in this area**? What do you want to understand or learn more about? Be interested, not interesting.

Show who you are—beyond titles

Here's the obvious secret: Whether you realized it or not, you began establishing your personal credibility about 20 minutes ago when people started filtering in the room.

What were you paying attention to?

On a bad day, we fiddle with wall charts, huddle in the corner with a key stakeholder or send a last-minute text message. On days that are worse, we get carried away with each other, chatting and laughing in the back of the room. Bad idea.

On a better day, all the futzing and fixing is done. We're relaxed, happy to be there, and genuinely curious about people as they come in the room. We're hosting the party.

Beyond professional credibility, there's a key ingredient between facilitator and group that is often overlooked. It's what influence experts call personal credibility. Who are you beyond your title? Are you someone they want to spend time with? (We have a colleague who used to say he was most successful with the groups that thought he would be a great person to go on vacation with.) Most importantly, can you be trusted to really listen, to get where they're coming from and act in their best interests?

Even more than what you say about yourself, personal credibility comes from what you do. Right there. In the room.

Back office creds

"What if I just don't have the creds?" asked a junior consultant preparing for a meeting with a high-level client team. "What experience DO you have with this topic or industry?" we asked. He thought a long minute. "Not much. But I've spent the last five weeks in their back office reading thousands of customer complaints. I really have a handle on those." You can bet the executive team didn't. Including back office creds in his intro made him valuable indeed.

Stealth norm

Sitting in the Land Rover under the glaring sun of Serengeti

The first 60 seconds

In a colleague's kitchen in drizzly Dublin, Gil Dove, an executive coach, changed my facilitation–and my home life. "When you walk into your house at the end of the day," he asked, " how do you spend the first 60 seconds? ""Drop your stuff and call out a warm hello? Show your partner you're happy to see them with a kiss? Or wave them off to finish a call, jot a note, sort your mail?" What you do sets the tone. Hit it wrong and it's hard to recover.

National Park, we watched a troop of baboons. Next to me sat Liki Likindokoki, a superb naturalist and 25-year warden of Tanzania's national parks, including 13 in the Ngorongoro Crater.

"Do you see what's happening, here?" he asked. What I saw was grooming and shifting about and guttural baboon talk. I suspected he saw more.

He pointed toward a young male sitting on the ground. The male's eyes were fixed on the largest baboon, a huge fixture in the center. "That's the leader, the alpha," said Liki. The young male, never taking his eyes off the alpha, edged toward a nearby bird carcass. "The alpha decides who eats what, when," Liki explained.

All at once, the young male lunged for the bird. In the same blink of an eye, the alpha lunged for him. There was a loud scream, a tornado of dust and feathers flying, a heavy thunk. When it cleared, we saw the alpha sitting casually a yard or so from the bird, looking absently into the distance as if bored. The young male was cowed off to one side, glancing around nervously at everything but the alpha.

When work groups come together, there may be fewer feathers but there is a similar dance. Group dynamics experts could say a lot more, but the bottom line is this: under the surface, on the unconscious level, there is something primal happening. Your participants are trying to figure out: Who are these people? Do I belong? What's my role? What am I supposed to be doing? Will I succeed? Will they see my value? What's allowed—how much authority do I have? What about her? What are the limits?

In a well-established work group, many patterns are already set. Some help the group function, while others get in the way of what they want to achieve. For example, clients often tell us about the need to bust the hierarchy. "The more junior members of our team have important insights about why this effort didn't succeed. But they don't speak up in the large group. We need to make sure their perspective is heard."

The facilitation style of a previous era tried to deal with group dynamics by having everyone introduce themselves, describe their role and tenure in the organization, then do an "ice breaker." Later, after the agenda, the facilitator might scribe a list of ground rules and ask everyone to agree to use them.

This start was never a good fit for us at On Your Feet. What we do after the facilitator's quick introduction is perhaps only subtly different, but to us has quite a different feel and impact.

We want to give the group a physical, real-time experience of a productive, collaborative working dynamic. Rather than simply talking about group norms, they live them without even noticing that's what they're creating. (This is why I call it stealth norming.) We want to set up a certain level of risk-taking; group members stretch in front of each other and succeed, which fast-forwards their ability to learn together. We also want everyone moving around physically, to help let go of distractions and engage their whole bodies.

We start by giving participants a real reason to participate:

- *We're going to give you some tools to help you get the most out of this session . . .*
- *Learning happens through relationship, so we're going to do something to help you get to know each other in a different way . . .*
- *You've come from a day packed with meetings, conference calls, overflowing inboxes . . . so to help us all get focused, stand up . . .*

Then, we use a warm-up chosen to create a specific dynamic that will help during the session, stretch participants in an unexpected (but doable) way, and fit the time constraints (perhaps 5 to 10 minutes for short sessions, longer if you're together a half-day or more).

Here are some examples of the types of warm-ups we use. Because they are innately co-creative and require some risk-taking, improv forms can be ideal. They also happen to be fun.

- **Swedish story**—In pairs, one is the storyteller and one the word-giver. Getting a title of a story that's never been told from the facilitator or their partner, the storyteller tells a story. The word-giver throws out words that have nothing to do with the story, and the storyteller must incorporate the words. Switch roles mid-way, perhaps with the new storyteller continuing the same story. Model first, then play in pairs. Highly scientific fact: works best if everyone is standing.
- **Story of your name**—In pairs, everyone tells the story of their first, middle, or last name, or a nickname they've had at some point in their life. (If you really can't think of anything, try the story of the name you always wished you had.) Back in the big group, invite people to introduce their partner, telling the story they heard. It's quite amazing how these stick.
- **Three favorites**—In legible handwriting, everyone writes down three favorites on a piece of paper (yes, favorite anything—dark chocolate, biking to work, the HBO series "The Wire"). Take 60 seconds to run around and see as many lists as possible (because it shakes things up, provides new stimulus, and helps people see each other in a new way). Pair up, and collide items from both lists to invent new business ventures. For example, my dark chocolate and your walking on the beach could turn into a gourmet s'mores kit for beach bonfire builders.

Afterwards, we do a quick debrief to surface the collaborative norms they just experienced.

- *What did it take to play?*
- *What did you have to do to make that work?*
- *What did you notice?*

Remember to highlight what you believe will help them get more out of the working session so they have it as a mental anchor to refer back to.

What if they don't play?

It's a reasonable question. New clients, in particular, ask it often. "I can see how this approach works with (insert well-known creative firm or advertising agency here). But will it really go over with my engineers (or lawyers, or finance people)?"

Here's my best answer: We've used this approach with literally tens of thousands of people across a variety of industries over 10+ years of work in India, Asia, southern Africa, Europe, Central America, and the US. Across all of those sessions, we've only had one person refuse to play.

He was a Senior Vice President at one of the world's largest shipping companies. My colleague, Gary, was explaining the rules of Bunny, Bunny to his team. The Senior Vice President rolled his eyes, crossed his arms, and shook his head. "This is s___," he said.

As a facilitator, this is the moment your stomach lurches. You're tempted to do a convince-job and justify the game (or yourself). You might also be tempted to pull out a .45. Unfortunately, none of these instincts are very useful. Gary, much to his credit, stayed calm.

"People have different reactions to this game," he responded, "and that's certainly one of them. By all means, do what makes sense to you." The leader huffed out of the circle and busied himself pouring another cup of coffee. After an awkward pause, the rest of the team turned back to face Gary.

Gary did the only thing that came to mind. "The bunny starts here!" he called with gusto, picking someone in the circle. "GO." The team committed, playing heartily to the end and creating a keenly observant list of what it took to play, but with no mention at all of their boss's outburst.

Gary didn't refer to it, either. He simply included the leader

Get them moving

Educator Sir Ken Robinson says we have been teaching people from the waist up. "We focus on their heads, and slightly to one side," he describes. "We . . . look upon their bodies as a form of transport for their heads—a way of getting their heads to meetings." But science tells us intelligence is diverse—visual, auditory, kinesthetic, abstract—and interactive. All the parts work together. Our experience: Getting people moving helps them access more smarts and creativity. (Check out his 19-minute piece at the TED conference: http://www.ted.com/index.php/talks/ken_robinson_says_schools_kill_creativity.html.)

seamlessly as part of the group as they moved into the next portion of the agenda. Slowly, the leader relaxed, and his participation increased and normalized.

Over lunch, he stood to get the group's attention. "I owe you all an apology," he said. "The game this morning didn't fit my picture of what we should be doing, and I was a little outside my comfort zone. I blew up. But when I saw you all playing and having so much fun, I was actually a little jealous. The bigger picture is that I think I often have the same reaction when we're in the office, and that pattern prevents us from doing our best work as a team. I want to change that."

Pretty heroic guy, don't you think? We learned something from him. Deep down, most human beings really want to play and be part of things. They are also starting from wherever they are. And when people get uncomfortable or triggered, they may push back. That's an offer, and you can choose what to do with it. One option is to recognize the reaction, without judgment. Then, do something with it.

Something they can say yes to

For a cynical or highly competitive group, try a competitive game (requiring collaboration) or a sabotage speech. "Imagine you drank too much last night. You really don't want to be here. What could you do to sabotage the success of the day?" List these. Really go there. Then, describe the benefits of doing them: "Life will be easier; you won't have to change or stick your neck out . . ." Then, the benefits of NOT doing what's on the list: "You might revolutionize your industry, take on what no one else has tackled, inspire your teams . . ." Point out the choice is theirs. Really, it is.

Try This

First, think about your upcoming session. Put yourself in your audience's shoes: For this and other courses, what do they need to be engaged? How could you meet those needs?

Audience needs	Ways you could meet their needs
Trust the driver	
Know who you are beyond titles	
Be seen	
Know where they fit	
Know why they should care	
Get something of value	
Be changed	
What else?	

That was just the initial mincing and dicing. Turn the page to apply this to your official session beginning.

- *Establish trust-the-driver—What does the audience need to hear about your professional creds?*
- *Show who you are beyond your title-What can you say and do to connect with them personally?*
- *Stealth norm-Thinking about the dynamic you want in the session, the group's culture, and available time: What warm-up could work? What debrief will help them discover useful working norms?*

Remember:

- Be interested, not interesting.
- The session starts before the session starts.
- If you project confidence and are comfortable with what you're doing, people will stretch farther than you think they will.

#3 GET THE HEAD NOD

Twenty directors from an environmental consulting firm sat in a semicircle in front of me, with their advisory board—industry notables who had given up the Monday of Memorial Day weekend to fly in for the day-long strategy meeting Tuesday. The COO, Claire, had contacted me ten days ago about facilitating. She was smart and driven, the firm's work in sustainability was innovative, and the whole business had a sort of Wild-West-on-a-mission feel about it.

Five minutes before the meeting started, Claire pulled me aside. The background materials had gone out late, she said—Friday afternoon before the holiday. She'd left everyone a voicemail, she assured me, with a reminder to review them. I took a deep breath. I didn't know how important their holidays were to them, but I knew how important mine were to me, and I was guessing that this was going to be facilitation as an extreme sport.

Not only that, but I'd reviewed the background materials she had sent. I could see a lot of work had gone into them, but they lacked communication from Claire about the focus of the day. I knew that she wanted to walk out with new clarity about strategic direction, and new insight into staying competitive in a rapidly changing marketplace, but I suspected the 20 people here thought we'd be talking about their proposals for a new training department, management standards, and other initiatives that she'd included with her email. I wondered if I'd regret taking this job. To avoid mutiny, I needed to deal with the offer. I had to get it out on the table without derailing the day—which was already ticking away.

So after introductions and a warm-up, I began. "Claire has asked me here today to help you get more clarity about the big-picture direction of the business, including your ideal clients and market position," I said. "I want to start by checking my understanding of your needs and issues around clear business direction." I moved over to the flip-chart easel. "Here's what I think I know about you," I said as I began walking through points I'd pre-written:

- Your industry is moving quickly and your business is rapidly evolving. It's hard to feel aligned
- You have a driving desire to create positive impact around the issue of sustainability, and grow successful biz

- For some of you: Not moving fast enough! For others: There's a new direction every day! (Hard to know your role/find comfort level)

A few heads nodded around the room. I paused to let it all sink in, then continued:

- Lots of opportunities—all working on different projects with different clients—lack of clarity about what target market is and should be, and how to be most competitive
- Also excitement, passion, new ideas brewing—COO's been saying, "Wait until we have alignment!" (training department, online environment, operational/structural streamlining)

I added a final bullet point.

- Memorial Day weekend

"Last week, you got some big fat emails that you were asked to spend your Memorial Day weekend digesting . . . and you may not even have been clear exactly what we're trying to accomplish today."

Now the whole group was nodding, and smiling revealingly. I flipped to a new page and read the critical question written there:

- What else? What don't I know about your needs and issues around big-picture direction?

There was a brief silence. Then a woman's hand shot up. Without clear goals and budgets, she'd said yes to everything and overloaded her teams. Another hand. Unlike the West Coast, sustainability in Texas was in its infancy; a different market strategy was needed. Someone else pointed out they'd never talked about big-picture business issues as a group before—so this day was a good first step.

I captured these and several others on the flip-chart, then turned to face the group.

"Starting now, we have eight precious hours together," I said. "Staying focused will be a challenge with so many critical needs knocking at the door, but you'll want to make every minute count. Here are the issues I believe you will get traction on today . . . " I circled them on the list.

"Given the need to get clear about big-picture direction, what we won't do is discuss or make decisions about any specific ideas or projects. Claire will need to hold a follow-up—say, within a month—for evaluating those against the direction you emerge with today." I looked at Claire for confirmation, and she nodded. The group nodded their agreement. They were on board.

I took a quick look at the time on my phone. "OK," I told the group, rolling up my sleeves, "Here's the value I think you'll get from the next seven hours and fifty-eight minutes . . . "

How to make Penny happy

My colleague, Brad, is a great dad, and has a daughter named Penny. When Penny was 3, she was famous for walking up to strangers in restaurants. "Hi." she'd say, squaring off in front of them. If they were talking on a cell phone or paying the bill, she'd persist until she got their full attention. "Hi. Hi. Hi. Hi. Hi."

Our hunch: humans don't ever fully grow out of the need to be seen (and, in general, they get too little of it). They want to know it makes a difference they are there. Being seen lets your audience relax and take in what you have to say.

The reality in your audience's head is an offer screaming to be accepted. You don't have to give in to it or change what you're doing—although sometimes that's an appropriate choice—but if you want to engage your audience and create a shared starting point, you do need to recognize this offer and do something with it.

It's important to do this like a sleuth, curious and with the desire for understanding, but without judgment. It would have been easy to blame Claire the COO for late materials, lack of clear instructions, potential team resentment for working on a holiday, and the possible ding on my reputation as a facilitator. (Really easy.) But it's not useful. It's more effective in the moment—for you and everyone else—to stay in sleuth mode and focus on fully recognizing their reality.

We've noticed something: people cannot help but give you a sign when they feel seen. Our highly technical name for it? The Head Nod. When you're capturing people's reality accurately, heads begin nodding around the room. Because your audience sees you get where they're coming from, you gain personal credibility. Because a good head-nod step reveals the full picture of what's on people's minds, later, when you get to the agenda, it's easier to set expectations and make trade-offs. It also gives you ways to continue seeing your audience, by tying back to what's relevant for them: "This next piece should help with the issue you brought up, Frank."

Eye-rolling, repeatedly bringing up something off-topic, challenging the process . . . much of what we chalk up to "difficult participants" is really an attempt to be seen when they feel their reality has been blocked or ignored, misinterpreted or glossed over. Getting the Head Nod up front—even before the agenda—reduces many of the behaviors that can sabotage a working session later.

INGREDIENTS

A map of your audience's reality

Your tentative hypothesis of their perspective, including practical and emotional reality.

Filled-in blanks

Invite your audience to do this for you.

Willingness to be changed by what you hear

Flex when reality is different than you thought.

HOW TO COOK IT

Map their reality as you understand it

The simplest and most straightforward way to see your audience is what I described with the environmental engineering team: Put before the group a tentative hypothesis, "What I (think I) know about your needs and issues:" Keep it crisp, about 5 to 6 bullet points. As you've seen, we often use a sort of caveman language—shorthand that's easier to follow visually, which we can augment verbally in the moment. Keep these bullet points visible, ideally on one sheet of flip-chart paper or on a pre-printed chart, so you can refer to them throughout the session. (PowerPoint really doesn't work for this.)

It's tempting to stick with the practical reality, the widely acknowledged facts about their goal, role, or situation. That's typically safe, non-controversial, and not very exposing. It's also incomplete. A critical part of seeing your audience is to name their emotional reality, too. Here's the difference:

- **Practical reality**: Lots of opportunities—all working on different projects with different clients—lack of clarity about what target market is and should be, and how to be most competitive
- **Emotional reality**: You got some big fat emails you were asked to spend Memorial Day weekend digesting . . . you may not have been clear exactly what we're trying to accomplish today

Huffs

Remember the wall charts we described in How to Arrange the Kitchen? Ideal for mapping their reality and keeping it in plain view. Honestly (the gang insisted I add this) I'm so keen on these that everyone at On Your Feet calls them "Huffakers." (Huffs for short.) We do occasionally get calls from logistics coordinators in Schenectady or Wimbleton reading from their boss' supply lists and wanting to know what Huffs are and where to get them.

If the emotional reality includes conflict or tension, this can feel dangerous. "Look, if I really said what was true," a participant once told us, "I'd say, 'You might be feeling frustrated and cynical, because we've been late on our last three shipments. We've promised to do better but you haven't seen it yet.' But I can't say that. No way. They'll crucify me."

Well, they already know you've missed three shipments and haven't made visible progress on your promises. This is not news. Whatever feelings they have about it are already in the room. If you don't take leadership and acknowledge these openly, chances are good those feelings will get expressed some other way—a less productive way that will be much harder for you to deal with. You can either talk about it, or they'll act on it.

Invite audiences to fill in the blanks: What else? What don't I know?

On a separate sheet of flip-chart paper, offer only this heading as you stand poised with your marker: "What else? What don't I know?" There may be a pause. You may need to repeat and reframe: I haven't talked with everyone. So what would you add? What don't I know about your needs and issues around big-picture strategic direction? Clarify and capture what you hear in bullet points. Watch the room carefully; is this an issue for many with lots of energy behind it? (If so, you'll see the head nods.)

Wait just a minute, you might be thinking. Isn't it a mistake to let go of control so early in the meeting? What if they say things I don't expect or can't address? What if, once the floodgates are open, they just keep going?

Our answer to that is, once again: What if these needs and issues are in the room and you DON'T hear them? Either they'll make themselves known later in a way that's harder to manage, or disengagement and resentment will take hold and grow.

Warning: Avoid the BIG temptation to ask, "What else? What do you need to get out of this session?" That's too narrow, too soon, and creates misleading expectations. Instead, ask: "What else?

You

Someone once told us people are 4 times more likely to hear the word "you" than any other. Use it a lot. Not, "The upgrade is late," but, "You've waited three months past the promised upgrade date; you might be wondering, 'When will I get that thing?'"

What don't I know about your needs and issues around this topic?" Map the territory of needs and issues—so all are acknowledged—then later you can show which needs will be met, how.

I've had to relearn the importance of Getting the Head Nod many times. I still remember a half-day with the bright, hip young team of a 35-person music company recently acquired by a gargantuan international. We launched into what we thought would be energizing tools for navigating the rapid change they were steeped in. But it all felt . . . forced. Hollow. Lackluster. We knew something was wrong, but couldn't put our fingers on it.

A week later, debriefing with the leader, we took a risk. "Something felt off to us. What did you observe about the team's participation?" He thought for a moment, and then—almost as an afterthought—told us that there had been significant layoffs the morning we arrived. Our jaws dropped. Ten members of the original company had been transitioned out, including the founder's wife, who had been with them since the beginning.

This was clearly huge for the team, and we'd blown right by it. Why? We'd been too focused on our plans for the session. The leader had some responsibility, sure, but the big chance was the one we missed in the room. Imagine if we'd mapped the territory as we understood it and then asked, "What else? What don't we know about your needs and issues around navigating change?" We would have gotten the reality we really needed to work with.

Geraniums 

Which do you want to know more about: A plant, or a red geranium in a cracked terra cotta pot? Authentic detail engages us and increases credibility. Include geraniums-details about how you got the information: Yoshi was kind enough to talk at 5:00am his time to help me understand what he's seeing in the Japanese market, so I promised to buy him a great cup of coffee when we met here.

If you get to the end of the time you have for mapping the territory and getting the blanks filled in (plan on 8 to 10 minutes for both parts in a short session, up to 30 minutes for a large workshop), simply say: "I'll take two more," then move on. Remember, you're the executive chef here. And if you hear things you didn't expect, we have some strategies to help you deal with them.

Be willing to be changed by what you hear

One September a few years back my partner and I took a float trip down the Green River in Utah. The boatman's wife joined us;

their first anniversary fell during the trip and they wanted to be together. Chatting as we spiraled lazily below towering canyon walls, we discovered that when the boatman's wife wasn't celebrating her anniversary on a raft, she worked at Sundance.

"The hardest thing for me to get used to at Sundance was how Robert Redford started his meetings," she said. "He would lean back and meet the eyes of everyone in the group. 'My goal,' he told us, 'is to be changed by you. After an hour, if I have the same perspective I do now, we will have failed.' You should see people pull their chairs forward," the boatman's wife finished. "We have amazing meetings."

Be willing to be changed. The obvious question is, how changed? I shouldn't let a laundry list of needs and issues hijack my meeting—should I?

We once watched a facilitator do something brilliant. When he asked, "What else? What don't I know?" he heard something surprising. It wasn't that he hadn't done pre-interviews (he had), or published an accurate abstract in the program (he'd done that, too). In that way the universe will always be mysterious, he'd simply missed something. Big. So big that heads nodded emphatically across the room.

He paused. "This seems like a big issue for many of you." More nods. He paused again. "For how many of you is this the most important thing we could talk about over the next hour?" Virtually every hand went up.

Now, he happened to be well-informed about the subject, so he knew he could provide solid value. He walked over and turned off his projector. "I'll post this presentation on the intranet." He picked up a flip-chart marker. "The most important thing is to make sure you get what you need, so let's spend this hour on Q&A. What are the most pressing questions?" His session was rated the best of the entire conference.

Being this changed is many a facilitator's worst nightmare. In reality, it rarely looks this extreme. If you've done due diligence—pre-interviews, vetting "what I know" with someone in the inner circle, reaching beyond the leader's perspective—and something substantive and unexpected still comes up, don't get rattled. These are offers about what's real for the people in the room, and you still hold the pen and the clock. You are there to serve the group, and it's your job to make choices about the best way to do that.

Here are a few mini-recipes you can work with when you receive unexpected info:

- **Acknowledge**—Simply recognize, "With x, y and z, there is a lot going on for you right now."
- **Clarify**—Make sure you understand the issue: "So when I hear you say that, I think you mean . . . have I got it right?"
- **Poll the group**—They can help you prioritize. "Show of hands: For how many people is this issue critically important right now?"
- **Scope**—Simply describe what falls inside the session, and what's outside.
- **Reassign**—"I'm not the expert on this, but I'll find one. I'll set up a call to provide an update on these issues within 10 days."
- **Make trade-offs**—Before you get to the agenda, call a 5-minute break and confer with a stakeholder. Or, prepare to give the group a distinct choice. "We'll vote to decide what best meets your needs. Option A is to proceed as is, Option B will be to drop 'What Our Competitors are Doing' and add 20 minutes of open discussion on market differences."

Having mapped the full reality—what you know and any filled-in blanks—it's time to set expectations about the territory for this particular session. You can do that now, as I did with the environmental engineers, or wait until you get to the agenda in a few

The Martian trick

Some people can't help it: they default to fat words, which are safe, but not helpful. "Sometimes our communication is lacking." "We need to collaborate better." We ask, "So if I was a Martian and I landed in your office and saw how you collaborate, what would I see, exactly?" Go for specific behaviors-like a Martian would see.

minutes. (The latter buys you time to organize your thoughts or consult with a key stakeholder on trade-offs if needed.)

Other ways to see people

Posting and reviewing "What we know about you" is the most straightforward way to see your audience, and does work incredibly well. But there are many ways to do this that add surprise, variety, and a tactile experience. Here are a few we've used:

- **Rip up your best ideas**—To a room full of sales veterans: "We're here to talk about overcoming pricing objections, but we think you're the experts. Please take the card under your seat and write the best strategy for overcoming a sales objection." Pairing up, they have 60 seconds to agree on the best of the two and rip the other up and toss it on the floor. In quads, then groups of eight, the same . . . and so on until we've reduced down to the top 3 or 4 ideas, then hear those.
- **Stories on the wall**—For the advisory board of a business school, coming together to talk about fundraising: Their own stories about what motivated them to serve on the board are on huge printed posters around the room. They walk in and immediately begin a gallery walk of these moving accounts.
- **Paper clips**—For the leadership team of an advertising agency in the middle of being acquired: We give each an oversized paper clip, and invite them to bend it into a different shape. Then, another shape. Finally, we invite them to create a shape that expresses what's real for them around the acquisition, and hear from each.
- **Your image library** —Scatter images with a range of attitudes, textures, and subjects on the floor. Invite people to choose one that expresses, for example, team strengths heading into the next year, and a second that expresses what that team needs next to be even more effective. Hear these.

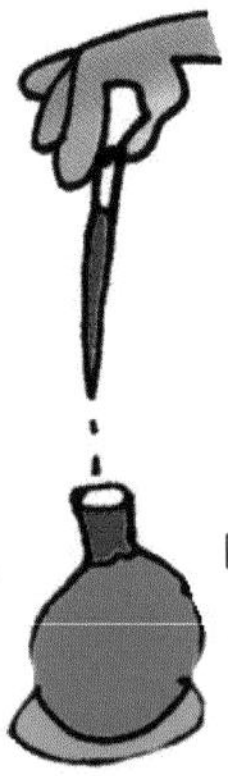

Try This

For your upcoming gig, sit down right now and brainstorm:

What I (think I) know about your needs and issues around ___:

•

•

•

•

•

Create a placeholder in your notes or materials: "What else? What don't I know about your needs and issues around ___?" (Of course, you won't fill that out now. Believe it or not, more than one person has tried.)

Remember:

- How can you keep "what you know" (and what you've learned) visible throughout the session?
- Did you include not just their practical reality, but their emotional reality as well?
- If you're not confident you'll get head nods, do pre-interviews, vet with someone in the know, or switch to an in-the-moment method like the image library.
- Remember to leave time for, "What else? What don't I know?"

#4 SHOW THE VALUE (DON'T TELL IT OR SELL IT)

Viewership was down. The new marketing director of a large national television station had gathered a cynical group of advertising sales reps to find new program promotion approaches that would really get people's attention. He stood at the front of the conference room.

We need to find new ways to promote our programs. I want to start our discussion today by telling you some things I'm sure you'll want to know," he said, clearing his throat and pulling a piece of paper out from his portfolio.

"The average crocodile has 60 to 80 teeth," he began reading from his script. "Adult crocodiles range from 8 up to 20 feet in length, and may weigh 2,000 pounds," he continued reading statistics, while the sales reps looked at each other in confusion, then disbelief, and not a little irritation. What did he think he was doing, wasting their time talking about crocodiles? What the hell?

The director droned on, then appeared to notice he was losing their attention. He faltered, "Um . . . lifespan of about 70 years . . . ," then stopped completely.

Suddenly, the door to the conference room flew open. Four wranglers with a 12-foot crocodile burst in. The huge croc thrashed and snapped, his muscular tail sending conference room chairs rolling askew as his handlers worked to keep him at the end of the room.

"I guess if you really want to know about crocodiles, you should ask these guys," the marketing director said to the gasping group, who by now stood teetering precariously on chairs pressed against the back wall. The director smiled and walked over to shake hands with one of the wranglers.

Recovering from their shock, someone started clapping. The rest joined. "We get your point," a sales rep called out. "No more talking heads!"

Showing really makes a difference—but why?

Using something visual, story-based, or experiential engages the brain in a completely different way than bullet points on a slide. Building this in early on—even before the agenda—intrigues people and creates buy-in.

John Kotter, in his practical book *The Heart of Change*, describes this process as "see-feel-change." He tells a great story: An executive, convinced he could drive down purchasing costs by $1 billion over 5 years, also knew it would require a huge change in processes and behavior by many people. To spark motivation, the executive collected samples of one item—rubber gloves—from across all company sites, each with its price attached. He piled the gloves (all 424 of them, prices ranging from $5 to $17) on a gleaming boardroom table, and invited the division presidents in. They immediately started picking through the pile. They compared price tags, first with curiosity, then astonishment, and finally outrage. In a few short minutes, they were raring to solve the problem of $17 gloves.

Kotter describes see-feel-change as a critical step in creating the urgency needed to drive change. What we know from working sessions is that when we give people a glove—when we show them something instead of telling them about it, especially if there's a story or physical experience around it—it makes them feel something, which compels them to roll up their sleeves and dive right in.

In their book, *Made to Stick*, Chip and Dan Heath also describe a similar experiential approach to making ideas sticky. They cite a brilliant press conference given by the Center for Science and the Public Interest in 1992. A spokesperson placed a medium bag of "buttered" movie popcorn on the table next to a bacon-and-eggs breakfast, fries and a Big Mac, and a full steak dinner. He made his point in an instant, and compellingly: Movie popcorn has more fat than a day's worth of artery-clogging eating. (Somehow knowing that only makes it more delicious.)

A facilitated session often functions as a mini-change effort. Including a "show" can help people absorb the value of the change quickly and remember it long afterwards.

INGREDIENTS

The value proposition

What's in it for them if they pay attention during the session or adopt the new technology?

A way to "show" it

An object, a story with vivid imagery, an experience, a video clip . . .

Connective tissue

Makes the point of your "show" crystal clear.

Chutzpah

Also known as courage, cojones, grit, or guts, it will help you do something different and unexpected.

HOW TO COOK IT

The value proposition: What's in it for them?

Begin by asking yourself that question. Thinking about the session itself, the technology you're focusing on, or the idea or approach being discussed or proposed—what's the real value for your audience?

What's in it for them if they influence the customer to adopt this new technology or take on a company-wide strategic planning effort? You need to hit on one that really resonates to turn it into a high-impact "show."

Think back: What was it for the marketing director's team? Moving away from the typical, boring "talking head" way of promoting TV programming creates possibilities for more effective—and more exciting—ways to get viewers' attention.

Choose your show

Get 10 ideas down. Don't self-censor—go for some terrible ideas. (If you can't think of any, call us. We've always got extra.) Try quick sketches instead of writing them out. It also helps to

Go deeper than money

Especially talking to sales people, it's tempting to say the big get is money. But money is always a proxy for something else. Dig past money for the value that makes their lives better, easier or more satisfying. It could be anything from customers that are raving fans to recognition from peers to more time to go to a daughter's soccer games.

invoke the "more heads" principle, and enlist a buddy or two with outside perspectives as brainstorm partners. They don't have as much clutter in their heads about this topic as you do, which means they will see things you won't. Of course, there's no right answer.

Now pick one with promise and develop it. How could you make it visual, simple, with a clear take-home?

Again, take our marketing director. He contrasted the talking head method of promoting educational programming about crocodiles with something he thought would really get his team's attention: a live one.

Skip the fog machine

Your show doesn't have to be elaborate. In fact, the simpler and more elegant, the better.

Finally, add connective tissue

Just plop a glove (or a crocodile) down and you'll confuse people; make both setup and take-home message crystal clear.

"We need to find new ways to promote our programs. I want to start our discussion today by telling you some things I'm sure you'll want to know," is what how the marketing director began.

Once his team was safely in their chairs, he drove the point home about which approach was more magnetic, and credible: "I guess if you really want to know about crocodiles, you should ask these guys."

He didn't have to provide the final punchline; his team took care of that for him: "We get your point. No more talking heads!"

Not long or cumbersome. Crisp and clear.

Here are some other crisp, smart shows:

- **Traffic vs. advice**—A group of sales reps came together for a course on creating engaging relationships with customers. We had them pair up and talk for:
  - 60 seconds about the weather
  - 60 seconds about something they had mixed feelings about
  - 60 seconds on traffic

– A final 60 seconds to get advice about something they were struggling with

"What was the difference in your conversations?" we asked. Then we confirmed what they experienced: some topics create emotional connection, others emotional distance. At the end of the session, they'd walk out with a number of engagement tools like this—common sense, but easy to miss if you're not paying attention. (This delightful exercise, by the way, comes from Roger Fisher and Daniel Shapiro's thoughtful book, *Beyond Reason.*)

- **Let go of agendas**—During pastries before a strategic planning session, we posted a big poster by the coffee pot. "Agenda: What do YOU think we should do in 2009?", it said. The team filled it quickly. A bit later, we had the group play Swedish Story (you'll remember this from the second recipe, Start with the Beginning: playing in pairs, the story teller has to immediately use words from the word giver in their story). Afterwards, the team described what it took to play Swedish Story: They needed to be flexible, let go of their agendas, and incorporate words given to them by others—which actually made their jobs easier, and took them to new places they never would have come to alone. We pointed to the graffiti page. "Your job today is not to convince others about the strength of your ideas. Your job is to let go of your agenda, and let yourself be changed by the perspectives of others. This is what you have to do to discover the best way forward for the company overall."
- **Don't get caught with your shorts down**—In a stuffy conference room in Las Vegas, a senior technical engineer told 30 global sales reps, "Here's what I think you'll get from the next 70 minutes." He reached behind a table and pulled out a 15-inch-high pile of paper. With a loud THUNK, he dropped it on the floor. "What you'll get," he said, "is that you won't have to read these. These are all the white papers about Internet security from the past 6 months. Your

A note about chutzpah

You need to feel comfortable and confident standing up there, doing this. If you're forcing, they'll feel it. It can take some time to get the hang of coming up with a good "show," but take heart: With practice, it gets quite easy.

customers have read them, and they want to know how the technology they have—or are considering—addresses the issues raised in these papers. If you pay attention, you won't have to slog through this stack, and you won't get caught with your shorts down when your customers ask smart security questions."

Now, imagine

You're running a 1-day meeting to help a nursing organization—a mix of union floor nurses and non-union managers—develop a model for shared leadership. Your session will take place several months before the next round of negotiations.

A key desired outcome is to walk out with a working list of collective values that can be used as guiding principles for both groups. They also want to walk out with a new understanding of how they could use these values throughout the organization to create meaningful new action that improves the standard of care.

Give these three steps a whirl:

- **The value proposition: *What's in it for them*?** Thinking about the session itself, or the idea or approach being discussed or proposed—what's the real value for your audience?
- **Choose your show.** Get 10 ideas down. Don't self-censor.
- **Finally, add connective tissue.** Make both setup and take-home message crystal clear.

As we've said, there's no right answer. Here's what we came up with:

Before the day began, we'd placed a bottle of Extra-Strength Tylenol or a bottle of Excedrin pain reliever in the middle of each table. (Due to group size—100—we had to use tables.) After the Head Nod step, we told the group we wanted to do something to show what we thought they'd get from this process.

We reminded them about the tampering tragedy of the early 1980s: someone outside the company tainted bottles of pain reliever with cyanide on retail shelves and put cynanide-tainted capsules inside, resulting seven consumer deaths.

Then, we gave them 10 minutes to discuss at the table: How did the company represented by their bottle respond to the crisis?

We began the debrief by asking the Tylenol tables what they came up with. Most remembered Johnson & Johnson's expensive recall and elaborate response, including removing all similar bottles from the shelves. They engineered a revolutionary new tamper-proof bottle, which became a standard for the industry, and enlisted 2500 people in a massive education effort.

Then, we queried the Excedrin tables. With some embarrassment, no one could remember anything about what the company had done.

We let them off the hook, confirming there was a good reason for that: Bristol-Myers (who owned Excedrin) had not, in fact, done much. They pulled product in one market that was affected. That was it.

We returned the group to the example of Tylenol, whose CEO later said he spent the majority of his time that year walking between employee desks and reminding people to let their decisions be guided by their number one value: "Our first responsibility is to . . . all who use our products." Today, Tylenol is the brand most trusted by healthcare workers—and has the sales and marketshare to prove it.

"Values shouldn't just sit in big binders on dusty office shelves," we finished. "Effective organizations use them to spur innovation, test priorities, and guide response during crises."

Show—don't "sell"

Don't cheerlead or coax. Teach by delivering new perspectives, information, and adding value.

Try This

Thinking about your upcoming session, or the product, process, idea, or solution you're working with:

- What's in it for them-what's the value?
- How could you show that? Get 10 ideas down.
- Which of these has promise? Develop it.
- To help your audience track, what connective tissue do you need?

Remember:

- Make it visual, use unexpected media.
- Keep it crisp and simple.
- Make it smart: Ideally, they'll learn something new that's of value.

#5 CREATE A ROOMFUL OF CO-FACILITATORS

Last summer I went on a guided hike in the Hoh Rain Forest in Washington State. The ranger asked our group where we were from, what we did for work, and what we ate for dinner. Then he told us the story of a young researcher he met when he first started working here as a ranger 20 years ago.

In cheap raingear, this underfunded guy trudged around collecting and analyzing the remains of dead fish," the ranger shook his head. "But he discovered something interesting.

"Most know that wild salmon return to spawn and die in the exact spot where they first hatched. What you may not know is that over 138 different animals and organisms feed on the remains of the dead fish, all within 100 yards of where they die. Analyzing the remains, our researcher discovered a new organic compound: Nitrogen 15.

"The next year, with a bit more funding and real Gore-Tex raingear, he found that N15 only exists one other place on the entire planet: in the giant Douglas fir trees of this temperate rain forest. Doug firs get their N15 from salmon remains. The Doug firs are essential to the survival of this rain forest—and this rain forest is needed to maintain an adequate oxygen supply on Earth. So based on his research, to have an adequate oxygen supply we'll need to make sure enough wild salmon get back to die and decompose where they're supposed to." The researcher even proposed a law that to eat wild salmon you'd have to catch it, consume it and stay in the immediate area for 24 hours afterwards to make sure you left all your N15 behind.

"When we finish hiking the next 2.8 miles," the ranger told us, "you'll have a different perspective on the dinner you eat tonight." He described the distinct ecosystems we'd walk through, how much time we'd spend in each. Finally, he said we'd poke around in a dry glacial streambed, where salmon hibernate, before returning to the ranger station at 5pm. He suggested we use the restroom, since there weren't any along the way and we wouldn't be stopping.

"Take a minute now to think forward to 6:30pm tonight, when you'll sit down to dinner. What's on your plate?" he paused. "Watch for how it connects to the natural cycles in the rain forest and how the rain forest impacts your life back at home."

"One more thing before we head out," he added. "I want you to get really good at an old Navy trick. There will be many hikers on the trail, and we're a big group. When you see a hiker coming, yell, 'Make a hole!' the way we used to do when a sailor needed to get through the mess hall quickly aboard ship," he said. "Yell really loud, so everyone can hear. Then we'll all squeeze right to the edge of the trail and let the hiker pass through the middle. We want them to get through quickly and easily so we're not distracted from our discoveries and they get by without anyone damaging the forest floor." We practiced, then set off into the forest.

This hike belongs to everyone

What struck me was how excited I was at this point to get hiking. I'll admit it: I had been grudgingly dragged from a riverside campsite and a trashy detective novel to take this hike. But now I was hooked. It seemed like this hike was created for ME so I could learn more about MY dinner. I think we all felt that way.

How did he do that? Well, the ranger had given us a personal reason to care. And then he made us co-creators of the experience, officially. Sure, he was the guy in the Smokey Bear outfit, and he held the boundaries of the agenda—a guided 2.8-mile hike through different ecosystems, we'd stay on the trail, we'd be back at 5.

But the ranger paid keen attention to our input all along the way and never stopped serving the group. Establishing what parameters were fixed created a lot of freedom during the hike itself. We watched him make scores of micro-decisions while still managing the larger agenda and timeframe—he stayed at some sites longer, skipped others, and sent us looking for pine cones or nurse logs to involve us in finding the answers to questions. He co-created with the group to serve our needs as he went along—but all within the structure he'd established.

He also made it very clear that we had a role in our own learning. He gave us a job. Specifically, we became stewards of our experience through the way we took care of other hikers on the trail. This snapped us into active mode in real, immediate way. A 76-year-old, a 7-year-old—everyone embraced the job, calling out "Make a hole!" enthusiastically, in loud voices. We felt like full participants with an important responsibility, and the ranger didn't have to use his time and attention watching for hikers, wrangling us to the edge of the trail . . . which would have been far less efficient. A colleague of ours, Sean Kinley, calls this "making people responsible for their own learning." He is very explicit about it. At the beginning of a workshop, he'll say: "My job is to . . . Your job is to . . . ."

Here's the deal: the groups that ask us in often desperately want us to make magic happen for them. And we don't fault anyone for that desire to have someone just swoop in and resolve their issue. So much easier! But even if you could deliver a perfectly baked solution to their immediate need, that wouldn't actually do them any favors in the long run. While your visible job as a facilitator is to help a group learn or problem-solve about a specific topic, your invisible superhero real job is to help the group access their own intelligence to find their way forward around this topic and others in the future, to help them feel more empowered and more courageous tackling the real stuff that seems daunting.

This recipe will give you ideas about what to say or do with a group to focus them, to make them responsible for their own learning—to enroll them as very active participants, even co-facilitators, to make your job easier and help them get the results they need.

INGREDIENTS

A connection between desired outcomes and the agenda

Clearly bullet what they will walk out with. Talk through the main beats of how they'll get there.

A "bike rack"—and a few other tools to manage scope

Charge the group with helping you identify and disposition important but out-of-scope topics that come up. When you make changes or trade-offs based on their input, make those visible.

Housekeeping

Give the group what they need to be physically comfortable—including location of restrooms and beverages.

A real job

Focus the group on something real that will engage them actively in taking responsibility for their own learning—a job to do along the way (to share responsibility for the process) or a real situation to apply new learnings to (so they have responsibility for finding a way forward).

HOW TO COOK IT

Connect the desired objectives to your plan for the session

Sometimes we call this process "linking" because you're linking what they care about with what you'll do. It's a quick but key step to help people feel oriented and know what to expect from the session.

- *With your needs and issues in mind, specifically what you'll walk out with today is . . .* Walk through the desired outcomes for your session, established way back there in the first dish, "Start with the Ending." (Remember, for best results, no more than three.)

- *What we'll do together to help you get that is . . .* Walk through the agenda, with key beats, time slots, lunch, and breaks. This is the place to set expectations about the scope of the session. You might . . .
  - Highlight agenda trade-offs: *Because we heard there are significant differences in what you're encountering across markets, James and I had a huddle and decided to spend 30 minutes longer with the competitive analysis so we can look at each region separately. This means we'll take 30 minutes away from . . .*
  - If needed, clarify what will NOT be covered. *With just one day, we are not getting into budgets at all.*

See them (again)

Use what you heard—and still have up on the wall—from your "head nod" step: "Jodi, this section will help you all begin to know which projects to say yes to and which may not be a good fit for the company's direction."

Manage scope with a bike rack

We were working with a client team that got together infrequently, and had gotten a flurry of email requests to include varying items on the agenda—none of which supported the actual desired outcomes. Anticipating that even more of these might pop up during the session, we suggested the team leader create a parking lot or a bike rack right up front, and use this to capture important but out-of-scope issues so they didn't derail the meeting.

"Oh yeah, we usually do that," the team leader told us. "We call it a bin list." This immediately brought to mind our British colleagues talking about rubbish bins on trash pickup day. We became suspicious.

"What do you do with the list?" we asked.

"Oh, nothing really," he said. "We just make the list. The facilitator's supposed to do something with it afterwards, but we never hear anything more about it. They probably just throw it away."

There is no better way than this black hole to communicate to participants that their needs and issues don't matter. If you want to maintain engagement and credibility, whatever you call this list, come back to it.

After we walk through the agenda, we usually put a piece of flipchart paper up on the wall and say something like:

Issues and needs may come up that are important for the team, but outside the scope of what we have time for today. If you hear one of these, please call it out and we'll get it up on the bike rack so you won't lose track of it. We'll return to this list at the end of the day and identify what actions are needed, who will do what, and by when.

It's important not to leave the room without taking this last step: clarity on who will address what on the list and how.

Do the housekeeping

People usually can't relax until they know their basic needs will be met. (This small step also helps reinforce the trust-the-driver you've established.)

- *We know you'll get the most out of this if you're comfortable and focused, so a few things that may help with that are . . .* Describe where bathrooms and beverages are, when they can count on checking cell phones, how they can let you know if the room temperature goes wacky, etc.

Give them a (real) job

This helps enact the shift from passive to active, and endows participants with the primary responsibility, from the start, for getting the results they want.

Make it real

Doing what the ranger did when he had us imagine our own dinner plates not only tied the session to something we cared about but also seemed to awaken a certain immediate, visceral intelligence. I had a big aha moment about the difference this makes during one workshop where I started out NOT doing it.

I was working with a team of leaders to create a communication strategy around an imminent reorg, with layoffs. The first hour, we'd filled a flip-chart with the bullet-pointed message they wanted to use at an all-staff meeting announcing the change. They were satisfied, but I had a bad feeling in my stomach. I just didn't buy it—too rah-rah. When I put myself on the receiving end, "promising future" and "valuable contribution" didn't address the real concerns I had as an employee: Would this reorg really work? Why was this the right answer? Was my job secure? Is this company a good place to spend the next phase of my career, or I should dust off my resume?

They, however, believed their messaging was adequate and were ready to get on with it.

So I did what any reasonable facilitator does when they have no idea what to do. I sent them on a break.

When we resumed, I asked each person to write down the names of three employees who were not being let go, were key to the company's future, and whom they wanted to keep engaged and motivated. Imagine your job is to have a one-to-one with each to deliver this message, I said. How would the three people on your list react? What else would they need to hear to feel reassured and stay committed?

An hour later, we had a very different set of bullet points. We also had a multi-pronged strategy that included monthly progress reports and one-to-one coffee meetings with the key players. These would serve as pulse-checks and important opportunities for assuring those who remained had a bright future with the firm. (Which they ultimately did.)

It was obvious in retrospect; I should have started with their real stuff—the real individuals they needed to have real conversations with. Focusing on real stuff moves you from the well-meaning but misleading, "Looks good on paper" to, "Well, I wouldn't actually say that" to the keenly accurate, "What they need to hear from me is . . . ." A different instinct kicks in, and it's super-smart.

Additionally, when a group identifies a real scenario or project where they plan to apply a new tool or decision, a sort of back burner magic happens. The subconscious mind busily beetles away, using everything the group is doing, saying, and stimulating to creatively problem-solve. Truly, the mind is brilliant in that respect. And it's efficient, too.

How you make it real will vary. Here are two simple approaches we've used:

- 4-1-1—Invite people, perhaps in pairs, to share a real situation where they want to use session learnings. (Ask them to be as focused as an operator giving a phone number and address—the 4-1-1 for a directory entry, see?) Periodically during the session, have people go back to their buddies and reflect on what they're learning about their 4-1-1—what's getting clearer, and what actions they might take as a result.
- Road test—As we started a session on decision tools, we told the team we'd take 90 minutes at the end of the day to road test the tools on a real upcoming decision, about how to staff a new facility. Their job as we went along was to identify which tools they thought would be most useful in upgrading their typical decision process. Throughout the day, unprompted, they tried tools out on their real decision. After a module on decision rights, for example, they asked each other: "So staffing the new facility—whose decision is it? Who gets input?" Etc.

Make them responsible

Like the Hoh ranger, you may also want to give them a job right there in the session so they're clear they are co-creating this with you and share responsibility for getting the results they want.

Recently, I did something I'd never done before. I literally invited a client group to co-facilitate with me, because I knew I couldn't get them where they needed to go on my own.

We met in Milan. They'd asked me to help with a prioritizing and budgeting meeting. The budgeting for the upcoming year was complex beyond simply applying strategic priorities. This manufacturing company was international, included multiple business entities, was selling some real estate subject to complex international taxation, and had a possible internal stock transition. All of this affected cash flow. And it made my head spin.

After a restless night's sleep in my hotel room, I decided on a straightforward solution. I'd get them to help. I got to the meeting room early and plastered the front wall, floor to ceiling, with flip-chart paper. Then, I created a visual map of the decision flow I thought we needed to walk through—leaving blanks to fill in the decisions and financial implications as we went along. On another wall, I drew some prioritization tools I had in my back pocket for us to use. No agenda, no time slots—only the clear need to have the entire wall filled in before we left that evening.

I held a short ceremony to anoint the group as my co-facilitators. I charged them with calling out what they saw was needed or missing at each step, picking up pieces I didn't see and making sure the complex considerations were all being addressed. I walked through the collection of tools, and encouraged them to suggest using any of them at any point.

About 10:30am, I heard it for the first time, "As one of your co-facilitators, I wonder if we're missing . . . " Over the next hours, there were many more. "As a co-facilitator, I'm wondering if . . . " "In my role as co-facilitator, I think we need to . . . " Together, we exceeded expectations for the day. Although we'd arranged with the hotel staff to have the room for "as long as it took," we'd successfully filled in the entire wall by 6:18pm.

Here are some other ways we've given participants a job:

- *Your job today is more important than mine: to be on the lookout for/figure out/discover . . . .*
- *Research shows that after a training session, the average participant remembers only three things. We are going to give you five tools. Your job is to choose the three you believe will have the most positive impact on your work with the team over the next month. (You have our blessing to completely forget the other two.) At the end of the day, we'll ask you to create an action plan using the three tools you chose, and share that with the group.*

Terrible promises

I make "terrible promises" when I anticipate people will get itchy. For example, "I promise . . .

- . . . this strategic planning process will have a beginning, a muddle, and an end. The muddle will feel uncomfortable–and really long!"
- . . . at times, some may get frustrated–you'll feel we're going too slow. Others will feel rushed–too fast. Different people have different styles; our job is to strike the balance."
- . . . moving from inspiring vision stuff to the nuts and bolts, you might get grouchy. That's normal. It can be overwhelming."

Try This

What will it take to create a roomful of co-facilitators in your session?

Desired outcomes: With your needs and issues in mind, what we'll walk out with today is . . . (you already have these from #1 Start With the Ending)

-
-
-

Agenda: What we'll do to help you get that is . . . (If you're thinking, "Wait! I don't know what my agenda is yet because I haven't designed the meat of the session!" you're right. Hang tight. That comes in the next section about creating real change.)

- Quick housekeeping: What do they need to know to stay comfortable and focused?
- Bike rack?
- Their real stuff?
- Their job-during the session and/or beyond?

Remember:

- Walking through the agenda, tie back to the "head nod" step.
- Highlight any trade-offs or things you're NOT covering.
- If you think the process will get rocky or uncomfortable, make a "terrible promise" about it.
- Come back to the bike rack at the end of your session and identify specifically who will do what, by when.

#6 MAKE REAL CHANGE

Cut back to Monterey. Tobey and I have just pulled on our referee shirts and whistles. "Don't get too comfortable in your chairs," we cautioned the group. "Our job is to keep things moving."

This will sound familiar if you are the kind of person who reads a book from the beginning. We started with this story. You may recall what happened next: we then launched into a series of mixed-industry breakouts with reflection and discussion in between, and as the rounds progressed, we used a variety of techniques to name external trends, identify strategic 3- to 5-year corporate goals and priorities, and capture the CIO's top needs and considerations pursuing those goals. Over lunch, speakers gave short teach pieces on five cutting-edge technologies and how early adopters were inventively using them. The day ended with CIOs rotating through a station for each online technology, working with the experts and each other to envision possible applications.

You probably also remember how three CIOs waved us over in the bar that evening and pointed out something we missed. And how, the next morning, we thanked them in front of the group and transparently inserted their version of the exercise, which produced rich and satisfying discussion. By early afternoon, the CIOs had developed potential technologies further, and self-organized around one they believed had the most opportunity to create competitive advantage for their enterprise.

And then, we gave them their last and most ambitious assignment: to "show" a short, live-action documentary from the future (read: these guys had to act everything out). Their "footage" had to show how the future technology worked, chronicle three giant steps needed to deploy it at their company, and show how they overcame a significant obstacle.

This assignment worked the way we'd hoped. Bringing their film segments to life physically accelerated their idea generation: "What if it had special functionality that . . . " "One thing we haven't thought about is . . . " "Try this—wouldn't it really help that user there if . . . "

And as they screened their documentaries, it became clear that the CIOs had fleshed out features, functionality and usage scenarios far beyond expectations. They programmed their cell phones to mimic new functionality, built things out of cardboard, climbed on chairs and dove under tables.

As they walked out that afternoon, change was already taking place. The CIOs had new insights into where they needed to take their enterprises strategically, and the roles they'd have to play. They had a new network of relationships to draw upon and were energized, inspired, and committed. The CIOs could see—in fact had literally seen, through the "documentaries"—the specific futures they wanted to create, and their minds had mobilized around needed steps and obstacles to overcome.

Learning by doing

What is it that creates the possibility for this to happen? When we're preparing for sessions, we hear the same thing from about 85% of our clients: "How can we make sure this really makes a difference? I don't want things to go back to the way they were. How can we maintain momentum and make sure this doesn't die?"

These are good questions. Workshop participants exist in a system—their organizational culture; the leader's strengths and flat sides; what they're rewarded for; their home life; their personal style, hot buttons, and appetite for doing something different. Their ability to "follow through" after a workshop is impacted by all of those. (And addressing them is a different cookbook.)

The shorter answer is that there are things you can do as a facilitator in your session to facilitate real change. Since all these courses work together to create an entire meal, it should be no surprise that some of these are embedded in other parts of the cookbook While every part of this cookbook until now strives to set up the conditions to create real and lasting change, much of what you can do falls here, in your core delivery section.

Here are the commonalities I notice when I look across sessions that have been extremely successful in creating real change (by now, some of these may seem a little familiar):

Near-obsessive tie-back to the desired outcomes. First and foremost, the core design for sessions that work been shaped by a sort of constant rigor. We are always checking back to make sure what we planned and did delivered on those desired outcomes in a way that created value.

A mix of practical and emotional learning. Often, in the design phase, clients ask us only for something very practical and business-driven. What we often notice is that a new level of self-awareness or some sort of emotional change is needed before they can succeed with the practical stuff. Imagine a group wants us to help them work on strategic direction. What we saw in our last meeting with them was they aren't listening to each other. We observed them voicing their own opinions over and over again, but not responding to or asking about others'. Before the strategic discussion, they need an emotional aha: to recognize each other as holding valuable—and different—viewpoints, and to be genuinely curious about and committed to getting these on the table. We might use an exercise where they need different perspectives to "win" or solve a problem; put them, personally, on the receiving end of different qualities of listening; or impose a "questions only" rule on a short discussion (and look at why that might be hard to do). Then their awareness will be raised as they listen to each other during the strategic exercises.

To get real change, you have to go for the emotional ahas first. Then you'll have better success putting practical tools to use.

Variety of experiences—especially whole-body. Our most engaging sessions seem to share a variety of who, how, and what—small groups, triad, pair, and solo work; games, different experience-based exercises, and simulations on real stuff; and a range of media (film clips, wall charts, objects, images). We use all of this to keep people's whole bodies engaged and both their right and left hemispheres firing.

I could hypothesize about why this experience-based approach works so well. Maybe when you're up and moving around and doing, you are laying down new neural connections and pathways—you are already being the change you want to create. Or perhaps experiences, because they involve senses and relationships, store new information in more places than bullet-pointed language on a PowerPoint slide that goes in only one mental file drawer called, "December 16th Team Meeting." But these are just hypotheses. If the science exists that answers this, I don't know about it. (If you do, please email me.) What I know for sure is that I see it work with our clients again and again.

A willingness to be changed as you go along. Looking back on notes from highly successful sessions, I often found myself saying, "Oh, that's not what we actually did. We changed that exercise because we discovered they needed . . . " or "Because after lunch we heard them say they were concerned about . . . " At first, I thought maybe I wasn't picking good design examples. After all, we had to change things, right? Then I realized the obvious: this was a design guideline. Part of the design work for the core parts of your session happens beforehand, and part of it is on the spot. In a good session, we use approaches from improv to stay in flow with the group during the session, paying keen attention to the offers they are making. This enables us to make micro-decisions as we go along to help them get even more value.

This applies to your picky eaters, too—the participants who seem the most difficult to manage. These simple (but not always easy) improv approaches can turn "difficult" offers into opportunities to make learning even richer.

Because there are infinite ways to design a session, I couldn't—and wouldn't—suggest a static set of exercises for great core design. You'll figure those out yourself. (I'm also secretly hoping the examples sprinkled throughout this cookbook from colleagues and clients have already expanded your toolkit.) The job of this chapter, like the cookbook overall, is to provide scaffolding that is robust and insight-driving enough that it helps you come up with your own brilliant, fresh, unique ideas.

INGREDIENTS

Strategy for each desired outcome, in a common-sense sequence

Plan one or more experiences, exercises, or guided conversations to nail each desired outcome. Arrange in the order it makes sense to learn them. Where needed, create time for marinating.

Practical tools and emotional ahas

Build in useable, everyday tools and extra skill-building or insight-driving experiences to create the emotional change needed to use the practical tools.

Variety of experiences

Involve both mind and body, right and left hemispheres, to enhance learning.

Real-time flow between facilitator and group

Notice more about offers in the moment (even "difficult" ones) and use them to refine instantly.

HOW TO COOK IT

To get to the designs that create real change, there's a short-cut—a simple set of questions you can walk through to help get all the ingredients in.

For each desired outcome: What experiences, exercises or discussion will nail this? What does the group need to do?

Options include—but aren't limited to:

- **A diagnostic**—to unpack and explore what's going on
- **A teach piece**—you providing information, or them providing it to each other
- **Generating ideas**—to come up with new possibilities or solutions

- An experience that drives discovery
- A conversation—with more, or less, structure to support it
- A practice module
- Something else you invent

Then, what's the logical order?

In general, session order is and should be common sense. If you were working through this stuff, what would feel right to you?

Sometimes, though, you want people to marinate on something. You might want them to marinate on customer needs and desires and come back the next morning to brainstorm new product ideas. If something is causing anxiety in the group—like how they'll hold each other accountable for action steps—you might have initial discussion before lunch to explore options and concerns and then return to it at the end of the day to refine a plan.

What else do they need to succeed? Any emotional ahas to put the practical into action?

At this point, we are going back through our initial stab at experiences, exercises, and discussions that address the desired outcomes, and adding in ahas and skills they haven't asked for explicitly but we see they'll need.

"Just-in-time" refers to a skill or tool that is not an explicit desired outcome but which is urgently needed in the room to move forward. Often, this is the emotional learning a group needs to be effective in working towards their practical objectives.

For example, we worked with a team that wanted their retail stores to be more "on brand." They thought they could accomplish this by brainstorming a checklist for retail staff, and enforcing accountability. We needed to show them the difference between saying what your brand is about and acting on your brand values.

Desired outcomes not what they appear

"Things are slipping through the cracks," the director told us. "My project managers (PMs) need to understand project flow and where they fit." We proposed a project-mapping exercise on a big wall. "We've done that. People just aren't using it." Hmmm. We asked her to tell us about a time when people "didn't understand project flow and where they fit." Her stories revealed the leader herself was drop-kicking urgent assignments without empowering PMs to reprioritize or renegotiate. The real desired outcome? An agreed-upon method for handling urgent requests effectively.

So my talented colleague Daryl hopped up and played an "Honest baker" sporting a t-shirt, signage, and promo materials that lauded his honesty (read: the typical brand manifesto and marketing materials).

Then, we asked them to direct Daryl as a baker who was in fact honest, but couldn't use the word: What would you see him do with customers, his products, with fellow shopkeepers, that would tell you he was truly honest? Tell customers the foccaccia really wasn't very good today, slash prices when the cost of ingredients went down, etc. Light bulbs went on for the team—emotional ahas. They got the difference.

At that point, they were ready to think about different approaches for engaging their retail staff in taking action to express the brand with more consistency and juice.

The power of a good debrief

Invoking our friend Thiagi again: "People do not learn from experience. If people learned from experience, my neighbor would not be on his fourth marriage. People learn from reflecting on experience." It's true. Your job is to help them make meaning of what they've experienced. A starter list of debrief questions:

- *How was that?*
- *What did you notice?*
- *What do you take from that about __ (topic)?*
- *How could you use that?*

How could we make it all more engaging and sticky?

At this point, we go back through our working draft once again, tweaking and enhancing.

Use grapples

One of our favorite ways to increase engagement and stickiness is what we call a grapple. What, you might ask, is a grapple? Well, think about the word itself. Grapple. What does it sound like?

If you're thinking a grapple is a wrestling move, or a hook tossed out to grab its target, or something you struggle with, you're close. We use the word grapple to refer to something that gets your audience to stretch for information before you give it to them.

A grapple can be an experience that leads to discovery, a multiple-choice quiz, a visual puzzle—anything that gets the audience to stretch, to work a little, before you deliver information. As soon as you introduce a grapple, you'll see the energy and life snap back into the audience's eyes. They realize they actually have to do something, so they reel themselves in and focus their listening to get the instructions. This increases engagement, interest, and retention, making information stickier. We often build in grapples at the beginning of a workshop module, and to highlight a key point in the middle of a longer teach piece.

Here are a few examples of grapples we've done or seen:

- **To start a module on influence skills**: We gave small groups 3 minutes to come up with the single best reason that would convince us to end at 4:30 instead of 5:00. They huddled in their groups and speculated, then presented their reasons—surely we were jetlagged, London was a great city to go out in, they'd give us even better scores on our course evaluations. "How did you come up with your reason?" we asked. Most thought about what would incentivize them or guessed based on what they knew about us. At last, we asked, "Is there anything else could you have done?" We could have asked you directly, one of the groups piped up sheepishly. (No one ever does. And people have the same tendency when influencing—they guess what will motivate stakeholders, but don't ask directly what they care about.) By the way, we did let the group go at 4:30.
- **To highlight a key takeaway from a teach piece about technology trends**: A side-by-side picture of a Model T Ford and a traditional steel mill. "I want to show you something that will have huge impact on your customers—and you—over the next 10 years," said the facilitator. He pointed to the images. "What do these have in common?" The group threw out a few ideas, and then he told them. "Both the auto and steel mills have gone through modularization. According to a team doing analysis at MIT, our industry is about to as well."

Build in variety

The brain thrives on change. We intentionally vary how people interact and what they do with their bodies and take care not to get trapped by PowerPoint or the flip-chart easel.

Assuming it supports the desired outcome, we'll use an interactive, on-your-feet experience over seated discussion whenever we can. Unusual naming and stories also help make information stickier. We use improv forms, show movie clips, hang big images on the wall, and have people bring physical artifacts to tell stories with.

Here are a few examples from facilitated sessions:

- **A 1-minute vent (vs. a PowerPoint slide with tips for listening better)**—In pairs, each person vents about something they're really ticked off about, with full permission to be as whiney and sniveling as they like. The listener's job is to listen, in complete silence, for what their partner cares about. Afterwards, the listener highlights, "You care about . . . What's important to you is . . . " The speaker gets a moment to add anything. The impact of this little gem from collaborator Karen Dawson? People are astounded by the power of feeling seen and listened to in this way, and of having someone hand the essence of what they care about—but aren't getting—back to them. They have something new and productive to work with. After being on the receiving end, people grok that there's something underneath the words and are extremely motivated to learn to listen for it.
- **The "five-finger method" (vs. a generic "decision rights model")**—Trace your own handprint and associate a different decision type with each finger (I decide, you don't get input; I decide, you get input; we decide; you decide, I get input; you decide.) When decisions come up, use this to quickly get clarity.
- **The Cleon story (vs. a discussion about perceiving things differently)**—My colleague Brad typed a long, detail-rich email to a client named Cleon. Within an instant, a succinct reply came back: "Good morning, Brad." He thought, good morning, Brad? All that time spelling out next steps and needed logistics, just to get this sarcastic reply? Didn't he appreciate the time that email took? Who did this

guy think he was, anyway? Brad asked his workshop group how they would have reacted, what they thought the client's motivation was. Their perceptions differed wildly. Brad then shared what happened next: After a calming count to 10, he wrote back a simple, "Good morning." This time, the reply was filled with productive, upbeat answers to all of his logistics questions. The initial "good morning"? Just a friendly greeting. People perceive things differently.

Maintaining real-time flow

I don't know about your family, but at my house you can spend all kinds of time preparing the meal, pour yourself a glass of wine and then—right when you sit down—a picky eater pipes up with a need you hadn't heard before. Your mother is allergic to something new, or your nephew has decided mashed potatoes are gross. The same thing happens during a facilitated session. Human beings are messy. The session will not go as you planned.

Avoid large group fatigue

A simple and important way to create variety is to change up group configurations: Pairs and triads, solo reflection, competitive teams, and groups rotating rapidly between different stations are all good formats to mix in.

Notice more offers—and use them

Think back to the discussion of offers in the Pantry. In our experience, to co-create effectively, you need to accept the offers coming at you in a way that maintains flow. You need to recognize and do something with them. Remember that offers are not inherently bad or good. They are simply information—stuff you can use.

In the improv world, noticing offers and using them is a rigorous practice for keeping things fresh and alive. When you're facilitating, noticing offers allows you to truly see your audience and maintains flow with them, building connection and co-creating to get to unexpectedly promising places. Your session will be more successful if you do a lot of it.

So the first thing you want to do is expand your noticing of offers during the session you're facilitating. When Cathy puts on her coat and shivers or there's a loud siren outside, recognize and do something with that offer.

Recently, we had a sales rep who was a huge jazz fan in a session on sales communication. Over a break, he told us about what jazz great Miles Davis called, "the crash that was heard around the world." A drummer wasn't listening to the rest of the band and crashed his cymbals at an awkward moment. It sticks out in the music like a sore thumb. We found it on someone's iPod and played it for the group as we talked about the importance of really listening to customers' reality. Accepting this rep's offer greatly enriched the conversation.

What about "picky eaters"?

For many facilitators, maintaining flow and receiving offers all sounds fine—until there's a "difficult participant" in the room. It could be someone who ratholes, challenges, has sidebar conversations, pulls out their BlackBerry, or needs to be an expert. They have just done something you didn't plan for and, frankly, don't have time for. How do you stay in flow with that?

It's worth noticing that we almost always cast the people who make these offers as villains. They are never the hero of the scene, or the helper who has a vital piece of information that will ultimately make the meeting better. We don't give them the benefit of the doubt.

Why not? As facilitators, we're already balancing a lot up there. We already feel like we're in the hot seat. When the "challenger" speaks up, it instinctively feels like it threatens our survival. When survival is threatened, people typically have one of three reactions: fight, flight, or freeze. We default to these reactive patterns before we've even had a chance to think about it.

If you didn't before, you now know that improvisers train themselves for just the opposite, something no ordinary human being in their right mind would want to do: when something scary, threatening, disastrous or frighteningly off-script happens, they run out and hug it. They accept and embrace it. Specifically, they recognize and do something with it. If you are on stage and a huge wall of water rises up and a writhing sea serpent pokes its

Just ask them

There is often a muddle in the middle of a working session. The group hits a big rock and gets stuck. You may be right there with them in the fog, stumped about what to do next. Try asking them:

- *What is clear right now?*
- *What is unclear?*
- *What do you need next to move forward?*

head out, the audience does not want to see you go back to the beach and build a vacation house (remember accepting and blocking? This would be a block—refusing to recognize it). They want to see you reach out, grab that serpent and take a bite out of it (this is accepting: you recognize and do something with it).

The biggest challenge for facilitators and other human beings is this: how do you accept offers when they're just plain a pain? When you can't or don't want to give in to what's happening?

- "Over my dead body will we spend money on anything else until we get more sales people."
- "This all sounds great, but I'm telling you right now I'll never do it until I see my boss doing it—and that will never happen."
- "Is this really the best use of our time?"

When you get an offer that feels difficult to deal with, the first thing we do is:

Recognize the offer—It's tempting to do what seems easiest in the moment: block that offer. If I ignore it, you're thinking somewhere in there, it will go away. One time out of a hundred, that might be true. More frequently—like Brad's daughter Penny—it will just get louder and more insistent. And if you continue blocking it, the group will start to get frustrated that you're not taking care of them.

So recognize the offer. Make sure the participant feels seen and you (and the rest of the group) really understand it. Clarify: "So what you're saying is . . . " "Your concern is . . . " "You want to . . . , is that right?"

Then, take a moment to notice more—Are people nodding their heads, or is the room silent?

One thing I've learned is that these offers are rarely ill-intended. They often spring from the unmet needs of the participants. Even understanding that, the question is, what can you do with them?

My experience is that 90% of the time, they fall into one of two basic categories: outliers and informants.

Outliers—These are offers that are specific to one or two people. Either they need to be seen, don't have the same background knowledge or needs as everyone else, or they have a particular style pattern that is disruptive (like habitually posing hypothetical questions or tangential concerns significantly off-point: "What I'm really wondering is, does an HR system exist to serve us, or us to serve it?"). Outliers do not represent the majority's needs, and detouring to cater to them would shortchange the group.

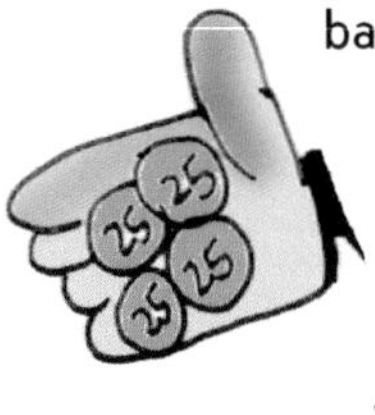

Informants—These people are telling you something. These offers are clues that there is something that hasn't yet surfaced but needs to be considered. They may come from someone who is speaking on behalf of the group, or is less afraid than everyone else to bring it up (even if the way they do it isn't very graceful). The solutions that want to be born usually look like problems first.

Remember you're there to serve the group. Ask yourself, "What does the group need in this moment?" You might instinctively know already. Or, you might need to poll the group to see if this issue is shared, and high-priority: "For how many of you is this a significant issue—show of hands?"

Now, do something with the offer—If it's an **outlier**, take the issue off the table and realign the group. "That sounds like a question worthy of a brown bag lunch—or a single malt scotch. If we talk about it today we'll have less time to look at growth options. I'm going to keep us moving." "It looks like only four of you are affected by this, so I'll continue with the original agenda. For you four, if you'll come see me after this session I can connect you with extra resources on the issue." After recognizing them respectfully, your job is to take care of them so they do not distract from group time, and refocus the group.

If it’s an **informant**, take steps to better meet the group’s need. “It sounds like many of you are concerned or confused about the decision process from here. Is that right?” Nods. Take a look at the agenda, and the clock. What’s possible? “Here’s a Plan B: We can spend 30 minutes getting clarity on this now and take 15 minutes off lunch and 15 minutes off our final discussion. How many would like to do Plan B?” Show of hands. The Plan B’s have it, and off you go.

Other distractors

There is also a host of smaller offers that run the risk of distracting the group’s process, like sidebar conversations, texting, or over participating. Although it may feel like these offers are sabotage aimed at you personally, that’s really quite rare. More likely, someone has a sick child at home, is trying to find connection with a co-worker, or isn’t self-aware enough to see the impact of their style and self-manage.

You can often accept these offers in small, subtle ways to good result.

Humor may do the trick

Brad tells the story of a flight attendant facing a plane full of passengers who simply would not get their carry-ons stowed and sit down for take-off. After several unsuccessful and stern announcements over the loudspeaker, she said in a light, sing-song voice:

“You’re still stand—ing . . . ” Laughter rippled through the plane and everyone buckled up immediately.

Start small, get bigger

You can also start small—accept the offers by taking action without recognizing them explicitly, and escalate to calling them out directly only if necessary. Here are some ways to start small and get bigger:

Sidebar conversations and texting

1. Physically move toward the talkers, continuing to address the group (they'll often stop when you get near).
2. Ask them a question legitimately related to the discussion to pull their focus back in. *What does competition look like in your market right now?*
3. *Let's have one conversation at a time, please,* or, *Are you with us, Dan?*
4. Call a break, bring the impact of their behavior to their attention, and make a direct request.

Over-participating

1. Change discussion formats, or issue a general reminder: *Now we'll work in triads and I'll want to hear from each triad.*

   To get full buy-in and make sure we have all perspectives on the table, it's important to hear from everyone. Who haven't we heard from recently?

2. Respectfully let the participant know you are going to call on others: *Alan, I want to make sure we hear from everyone, so I'm going to see if we have input from others on this one.*
3. Talk with the participant during a break, observe the impact of their behavior, and make a direct request.

If these actions don't have enough power, call a time out and check in with the leader. It rarely, rarely gets to that, however.

Reality check

Yes, there are crazy people out there—people my Dad would have called "diagnosable." But there are fewer of them in your workshops than you might imagine. (I've worked with over 8,000 participants and can think of exactly two who fit that description.) When they do show up, sometimes there's nothing you can do but minimize their impact until you can pull the leader aside and have a chat.

Accepting difficult offers effectively, with grace and clarity, is part of the personal growth of a facilitator. We each have our own individual learning curve. I once had a participant get out of his chair and do a yoga pose in the middle of a group discussion. At that point in my own learning, I simply had no idea what to do with his downward dog. (So, in fact, I didn't do anything.)

If as an individual you are uncomfortable with conflict or challenged to hold your own personal boundaries, your learning curve around this stuff may be steeper. "Difficult" offers can be terrific teachers.

Try This

Thinking about your upcoming session:

Desired outcomes (Again, from #1 Start with the Ending):	What experiences, exercises or discussion could get you to these?
1.	
2.	
3.	

- What's the logical order?
- What else do they need to succeed? Just-in-time learning? Emotional ahas?
- What would make this more engaging and sticky? Where could you add grapples? More variety?

And finally:

- How will you maintain flow with the group? What will you have to do to make that happen?
- What will support your ability to distinguish an outlier from an informant and take the most helpful action?

#7 END WITH SOMETHING STICKY

Dee Hock, founder of Visa International, once described a bank president he worked for who always ended his meetings with the same question:

"Has this meeting served your purpose?" the president would ask.

It was an unusual question to be asked, Hock noticed. It was especially unexpected when the bank president was the one who had called YOU in. He got the impression the bank president really cared about your answer, too. It filled you with a sense of . . . well, abundance . . . to reflect on what you wanted, what you'd learned, and what was next. You walked out with a sense of purpose and confidence.

This really caught my attention, so I tried it not long ago with a colleague. She'd asked to meet for lunch and talk about her personal aspirations to do significant travel. About 5 years ago, my partner and I set aside a year to be students of the world; for a remarkable, challenging, and thrilling 13 months, we worked our way around the equator on a shoestring budget. My colleague wanted to hear more about what it took to make that happen—especially the practical details like what to do about the cat, the mortgage, malaria, tax returns.

As we finished our lunch, I popped the question: "Has this meeting served your purpose?" (It felt orchestrated and bank president-y coming out of my mouth, not to mention self-serving—like I was asking for praise or appreciation. But I was curious, so I stuck with it.) The way she answered was a surprise.

She paused, took a breath—this is someone who normally moves a million miles a minute—and went inside her own head, thinking. Then, she met my eyes with a quiet, steady gaze and began talking. "Well, when I first called you I wanted . . . And what we've talked about has given me . . . What I've also gotten that I didn't expect was . . . So altogether this lunch has strengthened my desire to . . . And what I am going to do next is . . . ." She sat there, clear and smiling, literally radiating confidence and resolve.

What was clear was that the moment the question was out of my mouth, she took over, owning her own experience and learning, and setting her own next steps. Six weeks later, she had quit her job and planned her travel, and just a few days ago, she returned an email from Barcelona.

The power of a sweet finish

A recent statistic from the restaurant industry asserted 21% of diners decide to go to a restaurant because of the dessert menu. Because it's the last experience at the end of the evening, dessert plays a large part in making the meal—and certainly in making the meal memorable. You want to do right by those last 15 to 30 minutes.

Of course, the bank president's question alone, "Has this meeting served your purpose?" wasn't what compelled my colleague to quit her job and go traveling. She'd been simmering on this for a while. But there is an unusual power to an ending like that: it connects you to the vision of what you really want and takes you on a tour of what you've learned that will help get you there. It also reveals what you haven't yet satisfied and points your mind toward filling the gap. Answering this question leaves you with a sense of abundance and personal commitment to seeing through the next steps.

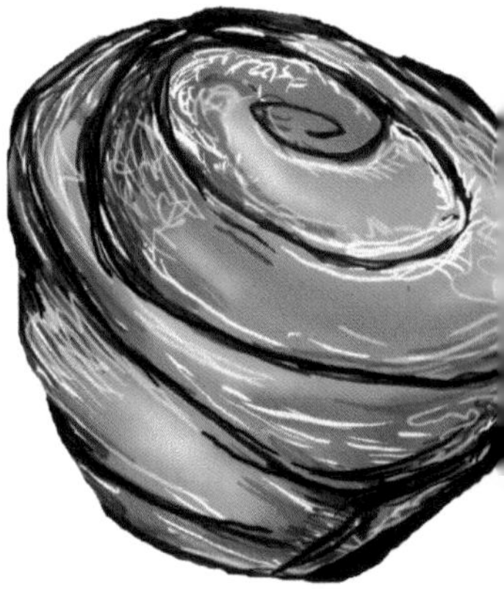

We refer to these as "sticky endings," both because there is sweetness and satisfaction in coming to the commitment yourself and because this type of commitment sticks more than anything someone else might prescribe for you.

Notice how this is subtly but significantly different from the traditional call to action of a sales presentation or the hurried (and therefore fuzzy) list of next steps from a planning session. It is based in individual reflection, which helps participants access the intelligence inside them that knows what comes next.

This reflection may not always unfurl in neat steps the way it did for my fellow traveler, but giving participants a chance to pause, uncover their own session learnings, and articulate the next steps they're truly committed to taking is a strong way to end. To experience an ending like this feels abundant and delicious. This is the feeling you want diners to walk out with after the meal.

INGREDIENTS

Recap

Tell them what you told them (better yet, have them tell you) and take care of any loose ends in the bike rack.

Ahas and takeaways

Create space for reflection—a chance for participants to make sense of the entire experience themselves, and compare perspectives with each other.

Next steps

Drive participants to get very specific with each other about how they'll take session results forward. What comes next?

Sweet finish

End with something delicious.

HOW TO COOK IT

Recap & empty the bike rack

Tell them what you told them. Remind them of the desired outcomes, and why any trade-offs were made. If you've storyboarded the room (see the Pantry), the recap will be particularly easy.

As we walk from chart to chart recapping, beyond describing what we did in each module or step of the meeting, we also like to highlight the specific observations, best practices, or decisions that emerged.

There are other, more engaging ways to go over a session. Some of our favorites include breaking up into teams to recap each section of the day in a lively way (we add constraints, like: must use visuals, must involve the entire group, etc.). We might also have triads show us what happens tomorrow in the elevator when they run into a colleague and she asks, "What did you guys do, anyway?" This gets the group to summarize what they did, agree on key messages, and walk out with one voice.

The tail end of the recap is a good time to tie up loose ends and take care of the bike rack. For each item, we might ask the group: "Does this still feel like a priority for the next 30/60/90 days? If so, who will do what, by when, to move it forward?"

Ahas and takeaways

There may or may not have been opportunity for individual reflection during your session. The end is a valuable chance for the group to hear how others are making sense of the experience—individual light bulb moments and lessons learned. It's also important data for the team leader or sponsor who's in the room. (This isn't meant to be spin doctoring. It's genuinely useful for all of them, and you, to understand what people took—and didn't take—from their experience.) As people articulate what's becoming clearer to them, those learnings become more explicit, more accessible and more memorable.

Relax

Once when I was in Bangkok, someone told me a joke. (At least I think it was a joke. Everyone in Thailand already looks so happy it's hard to tell.) "What three things should never run?" I was stumped. "Elephants, women in sarongs, and the King." Maybe I didn't laugh enough. He explained, "Walking, they're dignified. Everyone respects them. But running-oh, no! So awkward, looking like they might come apart! No dignity." Add facilitators. Rushing-especially at the end-simply does not look good on us.

You might use . . .

- **Stand by**—Literally, ask people to go stand by the wall chart containing what will be most valuable to them as they tackle the next challenge or take action in the 4-1-1 situation they identified earlier as their real stuff to work on. Clump up with others who chose the same thing and discuss why you chose it. Report out.
- **Half life**—Another great game from Thiagi: In teams, express the key learnings of the workshop in exactly 16 words. Hear these, then reduce to 8, then 4. You might ask people to frame the learnings as advice to themselves based on the workshop or as an elevator summary for the CEO who wants to know, "How did yesterday's meeting benefit the business?" Give feedback at each round about what's especially effective for their "audience" and let it be known they can steal, refine, or start over between rounds.
- **Learning buddies and the 4-1-1**—Return to the pairs established during Creating a Roomful of Co-Facilitators to share key ahas or takeaways about the 4-1-1 situation they chose to work with earlier in the session.

Next steps

In the elevator on the way up to a gig, a collaborator said to me, "I'm going to work on saying 'fabulous' less. I've been told my frequency with 'fabulous' is distracting, and can come across as insincere. Will you watch that with me, and give me feedback?"

She cited research showing that, if you advertise behavior changes you're trying to make, you're more likely to succeed. If others don't know what you're working on, they're more likely to see what they expect to see (the same old behaviors), and respond to those. Without reinforcement, it's hard to believe new behaviors are worth the effort—and they soon evaporate. Advertise what you're working on so others are more likely to see and support it.

Getting clear about what comes next, and advertising it with each other, may include:

- **Who needs to know what?**—Outside this room, what, if anything, needs to be reported back? To whom? By when? Will this happen? Avoid the need to deal with the rumor mill by walking out with a plan.
- **Clear next steps**—What comes next? Who will do it, by when? How will we check in and hold ourselves accountable? And sometimes: What happens if we don't?

- **New behaviors and piggybacking**—The word on the street is that new behaviors are stickier if people practice them back on the job for 21 days (some say 30, others 90). The bottom line is to focus on practicing a new behavior so it transforms into the way things get done.

Everyone's tendency, in the excitement of a workshop, is to pile new initiatives and action steps on top of what's already on their desks. When push comes to shove, new items fall off in favor of the critical priorities already in place.

What we call "piggybacking," or using an embedding strategy, is particularly useful here. Look for opportunities to address the same critical priorities that were already there differently.

Look for ways to piggyback new tools onto meetings, rituals, processes, and structures that already exist. For example, if you want architects to use a new set of design principles on every building, embed these design principles into proposals, project reviews, and post-project debriefs.

- **Individual commitments**—what will YOU do? Commit to taking action in a specific relationship (i.e., in your 4-1-1), approaching an upcoming task using a new tool, having coffee with your learning buddy for peer coaching, or a follow-up with your manager to realign performance goals.

Keep/ stop/start

Try a version of these questions: Based on what we've experienced here, to be as effective as possible next year . . .

- *What do I/we need to keep doing?*
- *What do I/we need to stop doing?*
- *What do I/we need to start doing?*

Group size, time, and topic will determine whether you hear next steps out loud. Sometimes we ask for a few volunteers willing to share theirs; other times we hear from everyone. For example, team members might take a few moments to reflect on the questions below, then, one by one, share their answers out loud with the group:

1. One aha or key takeaway for me is . . .
2. The way I'll take this back to my work with the team next week is . . .
3. I'll ask for support from . . .

Sweet finish

End with chocolate. This doesn't actually have to be chocolate, of course—although sometimes that's cool—but it should be something deliciously satisfying. You want that sense of abundance the bank president created.

You might have already done this by hearing everyone's individual commitments, which can be unexpectedly satisfying. Or, you might play a final, rousing game, end on a moving quote, give the team custom T-shirts or send everyone home with a book that builds on the day.

Try This

Create a sticky ending for your upcoming session:

- Recap-Desired outcomes, and what you actually did and decided.
- Bike rack-Which of these are still priorities? Who will do what, when?
- Ahas and takeaways-How will you reveal these?
- Next steps-Who needs to know what; what will WE do; what will I do?
- Sweet finish-What could you do to end with abundance?

Remember:

Piggyback next steps onto existing meetings and processes. Different, not more.

THE FULL MEAL DEAL

We didn't give them much time: 15 minutes, to design a 30-minute session they had to facilitate right then with a group of their peers.

They were a group of junior consultants at a global firm who often jumped in to run client sessions, but had no background or special training in facilitation. We'd spent a day with them working through the tools in this cookbook. Between you and me, we weren't sure they could pull this off. But what we saw humbled and amazed us.

Their session was simple and effective. Here it is, start to finish:

#1 Start with the ending—The team wanted to walk out with (1) new understanding of what's getting in the way of clients executing consultant recommendations more fully, and (2) clear next steps to increase the rate of successful execution.

#2 Start with the beginning and #3 Get the head nod—After brief introductions, the facilitators asked each group member to share a story about a time when their client had successfully implemented consultant recommendations, including what enabled this success and how it impacted them personally. You can imagine what began happening: participants began to connect to each other; get real situations, best practices; and gaps on the table; and develop a sense of optimism and commitment around solving the problem.

#4 Show the value (don't tell it or sell it)—In big numbers, the facilitators wrote "15%" on their flip-chart. "Does anyone know what this has to do with our topic?" they asked. A recent firm survey, they explained, showed that despite the millions of dollars and hours invested in world-class problem solving for clients, only 15% of team recommendations were actually implemented.

#5 Create co-facilitators—They then outlined the three steps they wanted to take with the group in the remaining time, and they set up a bike rack for extras.

#6 Make real change—The group broke into three small teams. Each team was asked to identify a real, significant project from the last year where recommendations were not executed. The teams each got a pad of flip-chart paper with "5 Why's" pre-written across the top, and #1 through #5 down the side. The facilitation team then told the teams to start by asking, "Why weren't the recommendations executed?" and to write their answer next to #1. Then, next to #2, "Why did that happen?" By #3, why that happened, and so on—five times. Then, the teams hung their "5 Whys" sheets in a line. They identified three core recurring issues, which the facilitators instructed them to title—like "The Isolation Cell" (project teams not soliciting input from client stakeholders, or not bringing clients along as their thinking evolved).

#7 End with something sticky—After a quick recap, the facilitators asked everyone to conduct a similar session with their project team over the next two weeks, and take a summary of these underlying issues to the senior partner in charge of the region. The group was still buzzing as they walked out into the hall for a break.

It just takes practice

Designed in 15 minutes, delivered in 30. An elegant, economical fit for the desired outcomes. An energized team made meaningful progress—and not just while sitting in their chairs having an abstract discussion. Clear next steps, and people motivated to take them.

They didn't need oodles of prep time or a full 2-day session like the one Tobey and I facilitated in Monterey to make this cookbook work for them. The session can be short. The preparation can be streamlined. In fact, as you practice using the recipes, designing and facilitating edge-of-their-seats-with-big-results sessions will get easier and more satisfying.

The junior consultants delivered a surprisingly transformational and effective session by combining the cookbook with their own experience and ingenuity. Now, you've got some new recipes. You already had your own toolkit, life experience, and imagination. So at this point, it should be pretty clear that the icing on the cake of this cookbook is a single ingredient. You.

YOUR HUNGRY TOOLKIT

Before you hit the kitchen, here are a few parting items to add to what you've already got going.

Our litmus test for what's included here: we've used it and found it exceedingly helpful for designing and facilitating sessions. What we haven't included is the mountain of individual articles, book chapters, and conversations we've found especially helpful when creating specific experiences and understanding human beings and organizations. You'll have to discover your own list of those.

www.thiagi.com—website for The Thiagi Group, founded by the charming and insightful Sivasailam Thiagarajan, which is packed full of resources for facilitators and trainers. We find the frame games particularly useful. Sign up for his newsletter—it's full of treats.

http://www.harvardbusiness.org—website for the *Harvard Business Review*'s online library. Rife with great source articles on different business strategy, leadership and organizational issues.

Made to Stick: Why Some Ideas Survive and Others Die by Chip and Dan Heath (New York, New York: Random House, 2007).

The Heart of Change: Real-Life Stories of How People Change Their Organizations by John Kotter and Dan Cohen (Boston, Massachusetts: Harvard Business School Press, 2005).

Retreats That Work: Everything You Need to Know about Planning and Leading Great Offsites by Merianne Liteman, Sheila Campbell, and Jeffrey Liteman (San Francisco, California: Jossey-Bass, 2003).

Training to Imagine: Practical Improvisational Theatre Techniques to Enhance Creativity, Teamwork, Leadership and Learning by Kat Koppett (Sterling, Virginia: Stylus Publishing, 2001).

http://appliedimprov.ning.com/—website for the Applied Improvisation Network, a community of practitioners and clients who are interested in the use of improvisation in organizations. Contains links to improv-based resources.

Everything's an Offer: How to Do More with Less, by Rob Poynton (Portland, Oregon: On Your Feet, 2008) (http://www.everythingsanoffer.com/)—I'll shamelessly self-promote On Your Feet by mentioning my fellow OYFer Rob's book. If you're curious about the practice (or practise, as Rob would write from his perch in the EU) of improv principles in everyday work and life, this book is an engaging companion. Rob is a super duper writer.

There are of course many outstanding resources we don't know about or simply haven't used. If you think we've missed something great, please tell us. Our toolkit has an appetite you just wouldn't believe.

A SWEET FINISH

Until it's possible to transmit chocolate via Skype, we hope you'll accept our offer of a few more recipes for some of our favorite treats outside the offsite. Because we're based in different places around the world, so are these recipes. Just Google "Cooking unit conversion" to get measurements you're comfortable with wherever you are.

Grilled Peanut Butter Slaw

You're thinking, "Peanut butter?" No, really. Seriously good.

—from Gary in Portland

INGREDIENTS

3 TBS	smooth peanut butter
1 TBS	rice vinegar
1 TBS	sugar
2 tsp	soy sauce
1	garlic clove, crushed in press
1/2 tsp	salt
3 drops	hot red pepper sauce
1/2 head	small green cabbage (cut through the core)
1/2 head	red cabbage (same)
3 TBS	vegetable oil
2	scallions diagonally sliced, about 1/3 cup
1 TBS	toasted sesame seeds, for garnish

HOW TO COOK IT

Heat grill to medium. Make dressing: Blend peanut butter and 3 tablespoons warm water with fork in medium bowl until smooth. Stir in vinegar, sugar, soy sauce, garlic, salt, and hot red pepper sauce. Set aside.

Place cabbage halves on a flat surface and cut into 1/4- to 1/2-inch-thick slices, slicing parallel to, not across, the core. Brush cabbage slices with oil, and grill until golden, 8 to 10 minutes, turning once. Remove from grill to cutting board and cut away core with very sharp knife so the cabbage falls into strips. Slice end pieces. Add to dressing with scallions. Toss well and sprinkle with sesame seeds.

Prep time: 10 minutes

Cooking time: 10 minutes

Makes: 5 cups; 4 servings

Pear and Watercress Soup

This comes from my lovely friend Toral, who teaches cookery—great fun sessions over a glass or two of wine with four or five others. The sweet of the pear is edged by the pepperiness of the watercress, an unusual combination that impresses. It's soooo easy to make and is delicious as a treat for those you love. Takes a half hour or so to make, and serves 6 as a starter or light meal.

—from Lizzie in London

INGREDIENTS

For soup:	4	medium pears, diced (skins are fine, but take out the core)
	1 bunch	watercress
	900ml	vegetable stock, (homemade if possible, but good quality cubes or granules/powder is ok)
	120ml	double cream
		juice of 1 lime
	1/2 tsp	finely chopped ginger
		Freshly ground salt and pepper
For Stilton croutons:	25g or 2 TBS	butter
	1 TBS	olive oil
	200g	cubed stale bread
	115 g	Stilton cheese, chopped

HOW TO COOK IT

Place two-thirds of the watercress leaves and all of the stalks in a pan with the pears, stock, ginger and a little salt and pepper. Simmer for 15 to 20 minutes. Reserving some of the watercress leaves for the garnish, add the rest to the soup and immediately blend in a food processor or with a hand blender until smooth. If it tastes too sweet here, add more watercress and pepper; also, you can use watercress and rocket (arugula) leaves. Put the mixture into a bowl and stir in the cream and the lime juice to mix flavours thoroughly. Season with salt and pepper. Pour all the soup back into the pan and reheat, stirring gently, until warmed through.

To make the Stilton croutons, melt the butter and oil and fry the cubes of bread until golden brown. Drain on kitchen paper (alternatively you could bake in the oven until brown). Grate the Stilton cheese on top of the croutons and toast under a hot grill until the cheese is bubbling. Pour the soup into (warmed) bowls. Divide the croutons and reserved watercress among the bowls and serve. Yummy.

Cranhorsey Sauce

Great with The Big Meal (a.k.a. Thanksgiving) here in the U.S., or on a sandwich, or with a spoon. I got it out of a magazine about 15 years ago, and do it every year. I hope that's not cheating.

—from Mame in Minneapolis

INGREDIENTS

2 cups	raw cranberries
1/2 cup	sugar
1/4 cup	horseradish sauce
1 TBS	fresh lemon juice

HOW TO COOK IT

Pulse in a food processor and refrigerate. Prepare at least one day in advance. Don't forget to eat the turkey too.

Oatmeal Cake

The preferred birthday cake for everyone in my family. You'll never go back. Outstanding for breakfast the next morning, too.

—from Julie in Portland

INGREDIENTS

For the cake:

1 stick	butter
1 cup	quick cooking oats and 1 1/2 cups boiling water
1 cup	each brown sugar & white sugar
2	unbeaten eggs
1 1/2 cups	flour
1 TBS	baking soda
1 tsp each	nutmeg and cinnamon
1/2 tsp	salt
1 tsp	vanilla

For the topping:

1 cup	brown sugar
1 cup	unsweetened coconut
1	egg
1 stick	melted butter
1 cup	chopped pecans
3 TBS	light cream

HOW TO COOK IT

The cake: Cut 1 stick butter in small pieces in a large bowl. Add 1 cup quick cooking oats and 1 1/2 cups boiling water. Let stand 20 minutes. Add 1 cup brown and 1 cup white sugar, plus 2 unbeaten eggs. Mix well. Sift together 1 1/2 cups flour, 1 tablespoon baking soda, 1 teaspoon nutmeg, 1 teaspoon cinnamon, and 1/2 teaspoon salt. Add to mixture, along with 1 teaspoon vanilla. Mix well. Pour into 10x13x2 inch greased pan. Bake 30 minutes at 350°F.

The topping: Mix 1 cup brown sugar, 1 cup unsweetened coconut, 1 egg, 1 stick melted butter, 1 cup chopped pecans, and 3 tablespoons light cream. Mix all together and pour on warm cake. (Suggestion: poke holes in the top of the cake using a toothpick first so the topping can soak on down.) Put cake under broiler to brown lightly (watch it carefully). Serve with vanilla ice cream. Oh, yeah.

Learning guarantee

If you don't learn something of value from this cookbook, your only cost will be a conversation. Contact us and tell us why, and what would have made this more helpful for you personally (julie@oyf.com). We'll send your money back, with appreciation for the feedback.

A Pollination House Project

This cookbook is a Pollination House effort. The Pollination House is an On Your Feet side project dedicated to helping get ideas that we care about out into the world. On Your Feet is a business consultancy that uses highly experiential methods—including improvisation—to help organizations with communication, creativity, and change.

The cookbooks are easily digestible, how-to guides for applying improv principles to specific areas we play with like facilitation, communication, change and ideation. They are loaded with specific techniques—recipes—we invite you to take and use. They also include plenty of examples, along with lots of tips we've learned the hard way.

Happy cooking.

LaVergne, TN USA
15 August 2010
193360LV00001B